Becoming a LEARNING SCHOOL

BY

Joellen Killion
and Patricia Roy

National Staff Development Council

NSDC is grateful to the New Jersey Department of Education and the New Jersey Professional Teaching Standards Board for their support in the development of an earlier version of this resource guide, *Collaborative Professional Learning in School and Beyond: A Tool Kit for New Jersey Educators.*

NSDC is grateful to MetLife Foundation for its generous support of the development and publication of *Becoming a Learning School.*

MetLife Foundation

This book was made possible with support of the MetLife Foundation. NSDC is solely responsible for its content and is not affiliated with the MetLife Foundation or MetLife.

Becoming a Learning School
By Joellen Killion and Patricia Roy
Editor: Valerie von Frank
Copy editor: Sue Chevalier
Designer: Kitty Black

Printed in the United States of America
Item #B423
ISBN: 978-0-9800393-6-8

"True learning communities are characterized by disciplined, professional collaboration and ongoing assessment. This is the surest, most promising route to better school performance, and the reasons are compelling. Teachers do not learn best from outside experts or by attending conferences or implementing 'programs' installed by outsiders. Teachers learn best from other teachers in settings where they literally teach each other the art of teaching. For this to happen, collaboration had to occur in a radically different way. ... Productive collaboration could not be casual or general; it was instead characterized by frequent, continuous, and increasingly concrete and precise talk about teaching practice ... adequate to the complexities of teaching and capable of distinguishing one practice and its virtue from another."

— Judith Warren Little, professor, Graduate School of Education, University of California, Berkeley,
in *On Common Ground: The Power of Professional Learning Communities*
(Solution Tree, 2005, pp. 141-142)

Contents

TOOLS ON THE CD

Acknowledgments

Becoming a Learning School began as the vision of Eileen Aviss-Spedding and Victoria Duff in the Office of Academic and Professional Standards at the New Jersey Department of Education in 2004. Working collaboratively with the New Jersey Professional Teaching Standards Board, the National Staff Development Council earlier created *Collaborative Professional Learning in School and Beyond: A Tool Kit for New Jersey Educators*. The book was co-published with the New Jersey Department of Education and the Professional Teaching Standards Board to address an identified need for more effective professional learning. "The Commissioner's Task Force on Quality Teaching and Learning recommends teacher professional development that is engaging, relevant to the work they do, more specific to their practice, and occurs closer to the classroom and within the school day. The concept of school-based professional development recognizes that the school is the primary center of learning and that teachers can often learn best with and from one another" (Killion, 2006, p. 8).

Since the New Jersey tool kit was published, the state has continued to improve policies and practices related to professional learning, recognizing that the state policy of accumulating hours to meet the 100 hours in five years requirement was not giving teachers opportunities to engage in productive and meaningful collaboration with their colleagues. Today, New Jersey has new standards for professional development based on NSDC's Standards for Staff Development, and every educator in the state has access to an extensive set of resources to support collaborative professional learning.

The partners who worked collaboratively to produce the New Jersey tool kit wanted to make it more widely available to all educators. *Becoming a Learning School* is the result. A generous grant from **MetLife Foundation** made this work possible. With the foundation's support, NSDC was able to engage the pilot and advisory team to offer guidance to produce *Becoming a Learning School*. I am grateful for the foundation's support of educator learning and its recognition that educator learning increases student learning. MetLife and MetLife Foundation's commitment to educators has a long history, apparent in the annual *MetLife Survey of the American Teacher* and other awards it makes to recognize and advance teaching and student learning. I am particularly grateful for the encouragement to make this resource guide available to all educators.

Significantly revised from the tool kit, *Becoming a Learning School* builds on the intention to provide educators with the resources to implement and support collaborative professional learning teams in every school focused on improving student learning. The development of this resource guide would not have been possible without the support of many people. I am indebted to a number of people for their significant contribution to this book. The writing, editing, and design team included four gifted people. **Patricia Roy,** NSDC senior consultant and independent education consultant, added her wisdom and practical and extensive work with schools, districts, and states to shape this guide. **Valerie von Frank**, eagle-eyed editor, provided expert advice and guidance in revising text and tools. **Kitty Black** contributed the design work that makes the book user-friendly and visually appealing. **Sue Chevalier,** copy editor, ensured that the final text is error-free.

Reference
Killion, J. (2006).
Collaborative professional learning in school and beyond: A tool kit for New Jersey educators. Oxford, OH: New Jersey Department of Education and National Staff Development Council.

The tools included in this book are drawn from a number of sources. Some are original and some are from other NSDC publications. Without the original thinking of those authors, this resource guide would simply be smaller. Their work makes this document more robust, resourceful, and rich.

Two other groups added significant value to the development of *Becoming a Learning School*. One is the **pilot team** (p. 3) of nine schools in Texas who had access to many of the resources included to try out and offer feedback for revision. Schools in Henrietta Independent School District, Allen Independent School District, and San Antonio Independent School District served as members of the pilot teams and were supported by their district leaders, Scot Clayton (Henrietta); Lisa Casto and Mary Clark (Allen); and Betty Burks and Diann Andy (San Antonio).

In addition to the pilot schools, a **national advisory team** (p. 3) met three times to provide guidance, perspective, insight, and expertise. All have extensive experience with collaborative professional learning and had many ideas to share that strengthened this work.

Vaughn Gross, NSDC consultant, skillfully coordinated the pilot and advisory teams, keeping them informed, checking in with them, encouraging their input, and providing excellent notes to guide the writing. She was indispensable.

NSDC Executive Director **Stephanie Hirsh** generated ideas for the original tool kit and provided guidance and support on its revision. A friendly exchange periodically occurred between us. She would ask, "Did you think about including … ?" to which I would respond, "It's in there."

NSDC's Learning School Alliance, coordinated by Director of Learning **Carol François**, will be the first user of *Becoming a Learning School* in its quest to build a national network of schools committed to implementing collaborative professional learning to improve student achievement.

It goes unsaid that a work such as this is a labor of love supported by the many professionals listed above. There are others, too, who support me personally. Prominent among my personal team is my husband, **Terry**, who was willing too many days to forgo dinner and a movie so I could work late into the night. As a matter of fact, he foraged his own meals many days and ate them wherever he could find empty flat space in the house. My next goal is to recover my flat space so I will be ready for something new.

To all, I am deeply grateful. — *Joellen Killion*

Pilot schools

Kendra Bennett
Principal
Henrietta Elementary School
Henrietta, Texas

Kristin Lennon
Assistant principal
Henrietta Elementary School
Henrietta, Texas

Quana West
Principal
Henrietta Junior High School
Henrietta, Texas

Gary Parrish
Principal
Henrietta High School
Henrietta, Texas

Scot Clayton
Assistant superintendent
Henrietta Independent School
District
Henrietta, Texas

Lianna Cano
Principal
Smith Elementary School
San Antonio, Texas

Maria Cordova
Principal
Poe Middle School
San Antonio, Texas

Linda Marsh
Principal
Brackenridge High School
San Antonio, Texas

Betty Burks
Deputy superintendent, teaching
and learning
San Antonio Independent School
District
San Antonio, Texas

Diann Andy
Senior coordinator for professional
learning
San Antonio Independent School
District
San Antonio, Texas

Johanna Walker
Principal
Marion Elementary School
Allen, Texas

Sandra McCoy-Jackson
Principal
Ford Middle School
Allen, Texas

Jill Stafford
Associate principal for curriculum
and instruction
Allen High School
Allen, Texas

Lisa Casto
Director of curriculum and staff
development
Allen Independent School District
Allen, Texas

Mary Clark
Assistant superintendent for
learner services
Allen Independent School District
Allen, Texas

Advisory team members

Amanda Alexis
2nd-grade teacher
Curtis Guild Elementary School
Boston, Mass.

Kathy Bade
Director of instruction and
professional development
St. Louis, Mo.

Marice Diakite
Principal
Patrick Kennedy Elementary
School
Boston, Mass.

Connie Jacquays
Director of instruction
Ohrenberger School
Boston, Mass.

Tricia McManus
Principal
Just Elementary School
Tampa, Fla.

Jeremy Mitchell
Assistant principal
Parkway Central High School
Chesterfield, Mo.

Odalys Pritchard
Principal
Adams Middle School
Tampa, Fla.

Foreword

Collaborative professional learning benefits students and educators. Educators must assess their instructional practices and their students' learning to determine whether the lessons they planned, the new strategies they used, and the explanations they devised helped students achieve what the teachers intended. Working together, teachers are able to assist one another in continually improving their practices, reflecting on and refining their work with the support of colleagues.

Effective collaborative professional learning requires everyone in the school working in teams and as a whole school to simultaneously improve the school and student learning. Effective collaboration around professional learning promotes the success of all students, not just some, as educators focus on specific areas of student need, driven by their analysis of classroom data. Effective collaboration promotes success for all educators within a school, not just some, as teachers work in grade- or subject-level, cross grade-level, and cross-school teams to focus on and increase their knowledge of their content and pedagogy. Because the school's whole staff is engaged in learning, this form of professional learning is sustainable and has a greater impact on achievement.

NSDC's theory of change stands on the assumption that students achieve more when teams of educators within a school and across a district engage in continuous cycles of improvement that focus their attention on their learning needs, as defined by student learning needs, refining their practice and accessing district and external assistance providers to support their efforts. Under this theory, educators do more than look at students' immediate learning needs. They build and sustain communities of learners to improve over time by developing their skills and their commitment to continual improvement.

However, effective professional learning communities do not just happen because we convene or assign educators into groups of learners. They take focused effort to build and sustain. They require structure, agreements, tools, and effort. School and district leaders, as well as teachers, have important roles in supporting collaborative professional learning that results in learning for students.

Becoming a Learning School provides the essential resources for schools and those who support them to learn how to establish successful professional collaboration at the team, school, and district levels. The resources in *Becoming a Learning School* will benefit schools just beginning to talk about collaborative professional learning and experienced learning communities seeking to improve student learning. This book is for both individuals and teams seeking to build learning teams on a solid foundation and those committed to refining and strengthening their learning, work, and results.

Learning communities focused on collaborative professional learning evolve and improve over time.

When successfully accomplished, collaborative professional learning teams have the capacity to address the significant challenges educators regularly face.

NSDC is deeply grateful to the MetLife Foundation for supporting the development of *Becoming a Learning School* and its dedication to making a difference in the lives of teachers and school leaders so that they can focus on their primary work, educating all children to meet high standards. The foundation effectively brings together organizations with similar interests and goals to enable them to explore unique ways to increase the impact of their work.

— *Stephanie Hirsh*
NSDC Executive Director

Introduction

At NSDC, we believe school is the center of learning for both students and educators. One of NSDC's fundamental beliefs is that schools' most complex problems are best solved by educators collaborating and learning together. Research increasingly acknowledges the added value of collaboration among educators as contributing to improving teaching quality and student learning. When educators learn together, we believe, student opportunities for academic success increase significantly. Further, we believe that the closer professional learning is to the classroom in which students learn, the more deeply connected it will be to student learning needs and student academic standards.

Like more traditional forms of professional learning, collaborative professional learning is defined by a set of standards drawn from research. Also like other forms of professional development, collaborative professional learning is results-driven and content-rich, focused on increasing student learning. What distinguishes collaborative professional learning from other forms, however, is that it is school- and team-

"If schools were to enhance their organizational capacity to boost student learning, they should work on building a professional community that is characterized by shared purpose, collaborative activity, and collective responsibility among staff."
— *Newmann & Wehlage, 1995, p. 37*

"Our view is … that if you can't make a school a great professional place for its staff, it's never going to be a great place for kids."
— *Hank Levin (in Brandt, 1992, p. 21)*

based, focused on the specific curriculum and the students that teachers interact with daily, and focused on those students' specific needs.

Many people have contributed to this movement toward teacher collaboration. We are deeply indebted to the research of Milbrey McLauglin and Joan Talbert, Fred Newmann and Gary Wehlage, Karen Seashore-

Louis, Sharon Kruse and Helen Marks, Anthony Bryk et al., Shirley Hord and her colleagues, Michael Garet and his colleagues, and the many others who have clearly established the powerful influence of teacher collaboration on improved school culture, teaching, and student learning. We are grateful to Rick and Rebecca DuFour and to Bob Eaker, whose work and writing for more than 20 years have made a significant mark on practices in schools.

Numerous writers have added their voices to support schools as they implement learning teams. The list is just too long for this space.

NSDC's work takes a slightly different orientation. We have shaped a new definition of professional development that stands firmly on the work of our predecessors and that clearly highlights the importance of professional learning. To support schools in implementing this definition and districts in supporting their schools' implementation, we have expanded on previous work for educators in New Jersey and Arkansas. This comprehensive resource guide is for school-based leaders, teachers, and those who support them as they implement NSDC's definition of professional development.

This book is the Sears catalog of collaborative professional learning. For those too young to remember it, the Sears catalog had all things for all people. It had tools and toys, stoves and stockings, dishes and dresses, linens and lawn mowers. Whatever anyone could imagine needing was in the catalog, described and ready to be ordered for delivery.

This resource guide promises the same. It can be used to facilitate the development, implementation, and ongoing assessment and refinement of collaborative professional learning in schools. It offers resources for classroom teachers, coaches, principals, and central office staff to help them understand their role in the success of collaborative professional learning. It is filled with tools to support the work of teams, principals, coaches, and central office staff.

HOW TO USE *BECOMING A LEARNING SCHOOL*

The book is designed to be an instructive resource. It includes hundreds of pages of tools on the accompanying CD and short sections of text designed to promote learning, planning, and action. It is both a map detailing how to launch, implement, and sustain school-based, collaborative professional learning and a tool to evaluate your progress toward success. The book can guide those just launching school-based, collaborative professional learning. For those in the early stages of implementing the process who want to strengthen their work, the book offers resources for expanding their efforts. Those already successful with collaborative professional learning will find resources for evaluating their efforts, introducing new faculty to the process, and extending and fine-tuning their work.

A good starting place is with the Learning School Innovation Configuration Map, included as **Tool 14.5** (on the CD and in Chapter 14 of this book). The Innovation Configuration offers users an opportunity to assess where the school currently is in its practice of collaborative professional learning. School leaders then can use the assessment to identify the best place to begin their journey toward successful collaborative professional learning using this book as a resource guide.

STRUCTURE OF THE CHAPTERS

Each chapter's structure includes these common elements:

Where are we now? These brief surveys allow readers to assess their perception of how their current practice relates to the chapter's topic. The statements ask for readers' level of agreement based on their experiences with various components of collaborative professional learning. One way to use the brief survey is to ask a team's members to respond to the prompts independently, aggregate the scores, and produce a mean score. After reading the chapter and using some of its tools, teams members might be asked to respond to the prompts again to explore the difference in understanding.

Chapter text. The chapter's text is brief and designed to be used in team and staff meetings to provide information needed to implement collaborative professional learning. The text is not intended to be a compendium of research, but rather practical information to guide practice.

Reflections. Each chapter ends with a set of reflection questions that can be used for discussion in team and staff meetings or for individual reflection on the chapter's text.

Tool index. A table describes each tool and its use. The summary table is a quick reference for readers to determine which tool might assist them with their particular needs.

References. Each chapter ends with a list of references for citations in the chapter.

REFERENCES

Brandt, R. (1992, September). On building learning communities: A conversation with Hank Levin. *Educational Leadership, 50*(1), 19-23.

Newmann, F.M. & Wehlage, G.G. (1995). *Successful school restructuring: A report to the public and educators.* Madison, WI: Center on Organization and Restructuring of Schools.

This resource guide is designed to assist the following audiences:

Audience	Use
Teaching staff so they can …	• Take an active role in learning with and from one another at school about issues related to their content areas, their students, their instruction, and areas of responsibility. • Share leadership of their collaborative professional learning teams.
Teacher leaders so they can …	• Contribute to the development of the structure, support system, and culture for collaborative professional learning linked directly to teaching and student learning. • Facilitate collaborative professional learning teams. • Develop teachers' collaboration skills and help establish structures for successful teams.
Principals so they can …	• Work actively with teachers and teacher leaders to provide the structure, support, and culture for collaborative professional learning linked directly to teaching and student learning. • Facilitate collaborative professional learning teams. • Ensure that teams have adequate resources and strategies to improve teaching and student learning. • Work actively with teachers and teacher leaders to provide the structure, support, and culture for collaborative professional learning linked directly to teaching and student learning.
Supervisors so they can …	• Facilitate collaborative professional learning teams. • Ensure that teams have adequate resources and strategies to improve teaching and student learning. • Work actively with teachers and teacher leaders to provide the structure, support, and culture for collaborative professional learning linked directly to teaching and student learning.
District administrative staff so they can …	• Support schools in creating collaborative professional learning opportunities that align with school and district goals. • Ensure that school staff have access to resources for collaborative professional learning. • Provide expertise and resources about content areas, instruction, assessment, data, and professional development. • Oversee the development of a local professional development plan that reflects the needs of individual schools and teaching staff and supports collaborative professional learning.
School- and district-based professional development committees so they can …	• Develop a school or district professional development plan that reflects the needs of individual schools and teaching staff and supports collaborative professional learning. • Use professional development plans from local schools to drive the design of district support. • Serve as local experts about state and district policy and provide research about professional learning. • Ensure that all teachers have access to high-quality collaborative professional learning.
Professional development providers so they can …	• Model collaborative professional learning. • Integrate collaborative professional learning strategies into all their work. • Support schools in developing collaborative professional learning teams. • Focus on the needs of individual schools. • Provide school-based support and follow-up to enhance transfer of learning and results for students.

Making the most
OF *BECOMING A LEARNING SCHOOL*

Readers of previous versions of this resource guide asked how best to use it. The following table shows specific questions others had about collaborative professional learning, with references to chapters that might be most helpful in answering those questions.

Question	Chapter
1. What is NSDC's definition of professional development?	1
2. We have professional learning communities. Is this something new?	2
3. How do collaborative professional learning teams differ from other kinds of professional learning?	2
4. What is the cycle of continuous improvement?	1, 9
5. What kinds of data do teams use? What about all the data we have from state and district tests?	10
6. Some teachers in our school are resistant to collaboration. How do we work with them?	4
7. We want to create a schedule that provides collaborative time each day, and parents are resistant to students being away from school more. How do we engage parents?	15
8. Are there ways to create a schedule for collaboration that doesn't reduce students' time to learn?	5
9. How do we create the kind of environment within our school in which teachers more willingly collaborate and see its value in refining their work and improving student learning?	3
10. What is the central office's role in supporting school-based, collaborative professional learning?	6
11. How can principals monitor and support teams in their collaborative learning and work?	7
12. How do coaches help teams, especially when there is one coach and multiple teams?	8
13. How do we organize the work teams do? How do teams decide what to do?	9, 11

Question	Chapter
14. What else can we do in our teams besides look at student work?	11
15. Who is responsible for leading teams, and what skills and knowledge do they need to be successful?	12
16. How can principals ensure that teams have clear goals, are working on their goals, and are making progress?	13
17. How can teams share what they are learning across teams within the school so that others beyond the team are benefiting from each team's learning?	13
18. How do we know if collaborative professional learning is making a difference in student achievement?	14
19. How do teams know whether they are working effectively and efficiently?	14
20. How can team members give feedback to each other about their contribution to the team without creating ill feelings?	14
21. Where did the idea for this book come from?	Acknowledgments
22. Did any practitioners review this book or try out the tools included?	Acknowledgments
23. Is it possible for coaches to facilitate every learning team in the school?	8
24. We have been doing professional learning communities for many years. How will this book help us?	1, 9, 11, 14
25. We don't know where to start. What is the easiest place to begin?	2
26. Where do we get new ideas if all the learning occurs in the team? Does this mean we don't have any other professional development outside the school?	1, 9, 11, 14
27. How can we plan to implement collaborative professional learning without meeting some of the typical resistance that comes when implementing anything new?	4
28. We have regular department meetings once a month. Why do we need to turn them into learning sessions?	1, 2, 3, 9
29. What is a SMART goal?	9, 10
30. How do we evaluate collaborative professional learning?	14

PART 1

What

is it?

Chapter 1

A NEW
definition

WHERE ARE WE NOW?

Teachers design professional development based on the needs of their students.

STRONGLY AGREE   AGREE   NO OPINION   DISAGREE   STRONGLY DISAGREE

Teachers learn in teams several times a week.

STRONGLY AGREE   AGREE   NO OPINION   DISAGREE   STRONGLY DISAGREE

Teachers' professional learning goals identify the knowledge, skills, practices, and dispositions to increase teaching quality and student learning.

STRONGLY AGREE   AGREE   NO OPINION   DISAGREE   STRONGLY DISAGREE

Professional development that occurs away from school supports professional development that occurs at the school.

STRONGLY AGREE   AGREE   NO OPINION   DISAGREE   STRONGLY DISAGREE

Principals and teacher leaders facilitate collaborative professional learning teams in our school.

STRONGLY AGREE   AGREE   NO OPINION   DISAGREE   STRONGLY DISAGREE

Too few teachers experience the quality of professional development and teamwork that would enable them to be more effective educators each day. As advocates for professional learning, our job is to make sure that what we know is essential to good teaching is embedded in all teachers' lives.

Good teaching occurs when educators are involved in a cycle in which they analyze data, determine student and adult learning goals based on that analysis, design joint lessons that use evidence-based strategies, are coached and supported in improving their classroom instruction, and then assess how their learning and teamwork affects student achievement.

Recognizing the need to ensure high-quality professional learning for every educator, NSDC is advocating for a powerful new definition of professional development based on this model of continuous improvement. NSDC is seeking legislative amendments to the definition of professional development being outlined in the reauthorization of the Elementary and Secondary Education Act, known as the No Child Left Behind Act of 2001. These amendments clarify which

This chapter is adapted from an article by Stephanie Hirsh, NSDC's executive director, in the April 2009 issue of *NSDC Policy Points,* a quarterly newsletter funded by The College Board for federal policy makers.

practices qualify for federal, state, and district funding, and specify NSDC's position that professional development should directly impact a teacher's classroom practices and student achievement.

Effective professional development affects many teachers as opposed to some, and many students as opposed to a few. The new definition calls for every educator to engage in professional learning at the school as part of the workday. Professional learning should tap the expertise of educators in the school and at the district office, with support from universities and other external experts who help local educators address needs specific to their students and school improvement goals.

Success in changing the definition of quality professional development does not depend, however, on including new language in the reauthorization act. When schools and school systems adopt the definition and alter their own understanding of high-quality professional learning, teacher practices and student achievement will begin to change.

The new definition of professional development is a moral imperative. The inequity in teaching quality and educational resources across classrooms, schools, and districts denies some students the opportunities for academic success. These inequities can be addressed through effective professional learning within schools. When schools become "learning schools," every student benefits from every educator's expertise, and every educator grows professionally with the support of his or her colleagues. Collaborative professional learning is a powerful way to ensure great teaching for every student every day.

Table 1.1 includes the elements of NSDC's definition of professional development, along with key points to support highlighted sections.

REFERENCES

Brandt, R. (2003, Winter). Is this school a learning organization? *JSD, 24*(1), 10-16.

Cohen, D.K. & Hill, H.C. (2001). *Learning policy.* New Haven, CT: Yale University Press.

Farren, C. (1999). A smart team makes the difference. *The Human Resource Professional, (12)*1, 12-16.

Fullan, M. (2000). The three stories of education reform. *Phi Delta Kappan, 81*(8), 581-584.

Garet, M.S., Birman, B.F., Porter, A.C., Desimone, L., & Herman, J. (1999). *Designing effective professional development: Lessons from the Eisenhower program [and] technical appendices.* Washington, DC: U.S. Department of Education.

Gregory, A. (1999). Solving the team-building jigsaw. *Works Management, 52,* 56-59.

Joyce, B. & Calhoun, E. (1996). *Learning experiences in school renewal: An exploration of five successful programs.* Eugene, OR: ERIC Clearinghouse on Educational Management.

Joyce, B. & Showers, B. (2002). Student achievement through professional development. In B. Joyce & B. Showers (Eds.), *Designing training and peer coaching: Our need for learning.* Alexandria, VA: ASCD.

King, M.B. & Newmann, F.M. (2000). Will teacher learning advance school goals? *Phi Delta Kappan, 81*(8), 576-580.

Leonard, D. & Swap, W. (2004, September). Deep smarts. *Harvard Business Review.*

Odden, A., Picus, L., Archibald, S., Goetz, M., Mangan, M.T., & Aportela, A. (2007). *Moving from good to great in Wisconsin: Funding schools adequately and doubling student performance.* Madison, WI: The Wisconsin School Finance Adequacy Initiative, Consortium for Policy Research in Education, Wisconsin Center for Education Research, University of Wisconsin-Madison.

Rothenberg, R. (2003, Spring). Thought leader. *Strategy + Business.* Available at www.strategy-business.com/press/16635507/8458.

Schmoker, M. (2002). Up and away. *JSD, 24*(2), 11.

Taylor, W.C. & LaBarre, P. (2006, January 29). How Pixar adds a new school of thought to Disney. *The New York Times.* Available at www.nytimes.com/2006/01/29/business/yourmoney/29pixar.html?pagewanted=all.

Yoon, K.S., Duncan, T., Lee, S.W.Y., Scarloss, B., & Shapley, K. (2007). *Reviewing the evidence on how teacher professional development affects student achievement* (Issues & Answers Report, REL 2007–No. 033). Available at http://ies.ed.gov/ncee/edlabs/regions/southwest/pdf/REL_2007033.pdf.

Table 1.1 NSDC'S DEFINITION AND KEY POINTS

NSDC'S DEFINITION	KEY POINTS IN THE DEFINITION
(34) PROFESSIONAL DEVELOPMENT— The term "professional development" means a comprehensive, sustained, and intensive approach to improving teachers' and principals' effectiveness in raising student achievement —	Several significant research studies in the last decade have concluded that the length and focus of professional development matter in its impact on teaching quality and student achievement. Yoon, Duncan, Lee, Scarloss, & Shapley (2007) found that when teachers have an average of 49 hours of professional development in a single school year focused specifically on the curriculum they teach, student achievement increases 21 percentile points. Other researchers, including Garet, Birman, Porter, Desimone, & Herman (1999) and Cohen & Hill (2001) found similar results for sustained professional development.
(A) Professional development fosters collective responsibility for improved student performance and must be comprised of professional learning that: (1) is aligned with rigorous state student academic achievement standards as well as related local educational agency and school improvement goals; (2) is conducted among educators at the school and facilitated by well-prepared school principals and/or school-based professional development coaches, mentors, master teachers, or other teacher leaders;	Because teachers have traditionally worked in isolation and pursued their own professional development, their learning has benefited them individually and the students assigned to their classes. Successful corporations build teams, and all employees feel accountable and responsible for the company's operation and success (Farren, 1999; Gregory, 1999). High-quality professional development that includes teamwork fosters educators' sense of collective responsibility for all students rather than individuals' feelings of responsibility for some students. Professional development conducted in teams creates an environment of shared responsibility.
(3) primarily occurs several times per week among established teams of teachers, principals, and other instructional staff members where the teams of educators engage in a ...	Professionals are responsible for continuously improving their knowledge and practice. High-performing businesses understand this. Randy Nelson, dean of Pixar University, the professional development arm at one of this country's most successful movie production companies, said learning is the secret to the company's success. "We're trying to create a culture of learning, filled with lifelong learners," Nelson said (Taylor & LaBarre, 2006). "Every employee is encouraged to devote up to four hours a week, every week, to his or her education." Learning is part of everyone's work. In education, continuous improvement requires that districts make time for teachers to learn and improve their practice during the workday. Many schools set regular learning time in before- and after-school meetings, early release days, or other scheduled times. When teacher learning is a priority, schools can find strategies to schedule time for it.

Table 1.1 NSDC'S DEFINITION AND KEY POINTS, continued

NSDC'S DEFINITION	KEY POINTS IN THE DEFINITION
... continuous cycle of improvement that — (i) evaluates student, teacher, and school learning needs through a thorough review of data on teacher and student performance; (ii) defines a clear set of educator learning goals based on the rigorous analysis of the data; (iii) achieves the educator learning goals identified in subsection (A)(3)(ii) by implementing coherent, sustained, and evidence-based learning strategies, such as lesson study and the development of formative assessments, that improve instructional effectiveness and student achievement;	American businesses compete for the Baldrige Award, which recognizes continuous improvement and associated results. While most schools believe in continuous improvement, they may not practice the process proven to produce results for students, including reviewing performance data, setting goals based on the data, implementing strategies to reach those goals, and then beginning the cycle again.
(iv) provides job-embedded coaching or other forms of assistance to support the transfer of new knowledge and skills to the classroom;	A preponderance of research in both business and education shows that adults exposed to new practices in workshops and team meetings need on-the-job support to make new ideas part of their daily routines (Joyce & Calhoun, 1996; Joyce & Showers, 2002). Odden et al. (2007) conclude that states that invest in classroom-based coaches who provide such support reap greater benefits in student achievement as opposed to those implementing more costly and less effective innovations, including smaller class sizes or full-day kindergarten. In addition, when experienced employees with a system-level understanding regularly share their individual insights about their company's processes and problems, they successfully build employees' knowledge (Leonard & Swap, 2004).

Table 1.1 NSDC'S DEFINITION AND KEY POINTS, continued

NSDC'S DEFINITION	KEY POINTS IN THE DEFINITION
(v) regularly assesses the effectiveness of the professional development in achieving identified learning goals, improving teaching, and assisting all students in meeting challenging state academic achievement standards;	Continually assessing professional practice and student learning can be challenging. Using formative assessments requires technical knowledge. Gaining this knowledge and using it effectively is essential to ensuring continuous improvement. School improvement specialist Mike Schmoker (2002) said substantial evidence shows that results are virtually inevitable when teachers work in teams to: • Focus substantially, though not exclusively, on assessed standards. • Review simple, readily available achievement data to set a limited number of measurable achievement goals in the lowest-scoring subjects or courses. • Work regularly together to design, adapt, and assess instructional strategies targeted directly at specific standards that students are not achieving according to assessment data (e.g. "measurement" in math; "voice" in writing; "sight reading" in music). Professional development and team-based learning must improve educators' practice and student learning. Educators must use ongoing assessments of their practices and their students' learning to determine the effect of learning teams' decisions. They then can determine whether the lessons they planned, the new strategies they used, and the explanations they devised helped students achieve what the teachers intended.
(vi) informs ongoing improvements in teaching and student learning; and	Michael Fullan (2000) said successful schools are places where teachers regularly focus their efforts on student work through assessment and then adjust their instructional practice to get better results. Few initiatives are backed by evidence that they raise achievement. Formative assessment is one of the few approaches proven to make a difference. Continuously identifying areas to improve, however, can occur only when teachers and principals have information about how instruction is affecting students. To have the information they need to determine where they have succeeded, where they may need slight modifications, or where they must completely change plans, educators need continuous evaluation. Continually evaluating practice and outcomes produces actions that lead to sustained improvement as opposed to incremental improvement or no improvement.

Table 1.1 NSDC'S DEFINITION AND KEY POINTS, continued

NSDC'S DEFINITION	KEY POINTS IN THE DEFINITION
(vii) that may be supported by external assistance.	Educators who are guided by data on their students and school are in the best position to identify what help they need to address their most important challenges. Occasionally, the school may not have answers and must seek assistance from outside experts. King and Newmann (2000) found that "ensuring the constant interaction of great ideas inside and outside an organization promotes improvement for all." When GE wanted to boost its leadership practices, CEO Jack Welch sought help from an outside expert, Noel Tichy. The result: an organizational culture developed in which employees embraced teaching and learning, emphasized results, and were able to adapt and change (Rothenberg, 2003). The company achieved its goals under Tichy's skillful guidance. Any organization that enlists external assistance, however, must ensure that the assistance aligns with the organization's internal goals.
(B) The process outlined in (A) may be supported by activities such as courses, workshops, institutes, networks, and conferences that: (1) must address the learning goals and objectives established for professional development by educators at the school level; (2) advance the ongoing school-based professional development; and (3) are provided by for-profit and nonprofit entities outside the school such as universities, education service agencies, technical assistance providers, networks of content-area specialists, and other education organizations and associations.	Teachers often criticize professional development for not addressing their students' specific needs. Principals' criticism is that professional development rarely addresses the school's specific needs. Traditionally, central office administrators plan principals' and teachers' professional development although they have limited capacity to specifically address the needs identified in each teacher's or school's student data. As a result, they design professional learning that may impact some, but not all, teachers. Some districts have allowed teachers to plan their own professional development, primarily by having teachers choose workshops or conferences to attend. This approach, too, leads to impact for some teachers and their students as opposed to more powerful approaches designed to improve the practices of all teachers to affect all students. Traditional professional development relies almost exclusively on outside experts and materials without integrating these resources into existing systems of peer collaboration. The intent of the new definition is to leverage outside expertise to inform and improve the practice of educators inside schools. The definition suggests that outside experts make important contributions, but the tremendous expertise of teachers within the school is required to determine their specific learning needs and then to seek others' help to address these needs. King and Newmann (2000) found that teachers are most likely to learn when they collaborate with colleagues both within and outside of their schools and when they access external researchers and program developers. Under this scenario, schools and teams become continuous improvement organizations, and, as Brandt (2003) states, true learning organizations exchange information frequently with relevant external sources.

NSDC'S DEFINITION IN ACTION:
MONROE TOWNSHIP'S PATH TO
CONTINUOUS TEACHER LEARNING

In the Monroe Township (N.J.) Public Schools, teachers' learning occurs daily, not just on one day in October or February. Central office and school-level administrators plan for and support job-embedded teacher growth. Teachers ask for and receive time to coach peers and observe in each other's classrooms. They meet during preparation time, stay after school to review, revise, and improve lessons, and implement lesson study groups. With structural changes that increase the number of professional development days for all educators and a cultural shift that fosters teamwork and collaboration, every day is a professional development day in the district.

But that hasn't always been so. How did the district become a system that typifies NSDC's new definition of effective professional development?

The district's path to continuous teacher learning started with extensive data analysis, including surveys of the staff about their learning needs. A professional development committee also studied research on what constitutes effective learning for adults and concluded that one-shot workshops should be limited and that the district should instead foster opportunities for ongoing learning by having work teams collaborate to connect learning to the work students do in classrooms.

The district shifted the structure of learning days, adding to the number of days allocated to professional development and releasing students early on others to give teachers more time for collaborative learning.

Transforming the content of teachers' learning was also critical. The district designed a differentiated structure of professional learning based on stages of teacher development, teacher interest, organizational goals, and research-based instructional strategies. Staff members have multiple paths for professional growth and have different options depending on their experience levels. Teachers in their first three years have structured learning options, while experienced faculty have more control over their learning based on their needs and the district's strategic plan.

The accountability and expectations for learning are much higher than before, and the results of the professional development have been impressive.

Christopher Tienken, former assistant superintendent in Monroe Township, said, "We saw an increase in the percentage of teachers who used differentiated instruction strategies, such as tiered lessons, and a large increase in the amount of student-centered teaching that took place in the district. Based on formal classroom observations and walk-throughs, we saw approximately 86% of the teachers using strategies they learned during professional development sessions and professional learning community time. That represents an al-

For more information about Monroe Township's transformation, including extensive survey data from teachers who participated, see Tool 1.4.

most 30% difference since the program started four years ago."

The district measured the effectiveness of the work, documenting progress along three criteria:

1. Participants demonstrate a positive change in skills, knowledge, attitudes, and behaviors. The new professional practice is integrated into the teacher's practice.

2. The desired changes and improvements are measurable and observable in both the short and long term. They become the norm until better knowledge or skills are available.

3. The results of the professional development lead directly to observable, measurable positive change in student outcomes on clearly defined criteria.

REFLECTIONS

1. In what ways are our current practices different from the new definition of professional development? Where do we meet the definition's standard?

2. What changes do we need to make to better align our practice with the definition? What policies would need to change? Who needs to lead the change?

3. What actions are needed to improve our professional learning? What steps are necessary? Who should be involved in that planning?

4. Who needs to learn more about the definition? Who should be responsible for informing others about the new definition?

5. As a team, what commitment will we make to ensure that we are using the cycle of continuous improvement?

TOOL INDEX

TOOL	TITLE	USE
1.1	Definition of professional development	Tool 1.1 is NSDC's definition of professional development.
1.2	Three levels of text	Tool 1.2 is a protocol for use with teams or a whole-school faculty in studying the definition.
1.3	How do we stand?	Tool 1.3 is a tool to help school staff assess where they are in relation to the definition of professional development.
1.4	When every day is professional development day	Tool 1.4 is a *JSD* article about Monroe Township (N.J.) Public Schools
1.5	Is and is not	Tool 1.5 will help educators clarify their understanding of how collaborative professional learning is similar and different from traditional forms of professional learning.

Chapter 2

COLLABORATIVE
professional learning

WHERE ARE WE NOW?

Teachers work collaboratively on the routine tasks associated with teaching.

STRONGLY AGREE   AGREE   NO OPINION   DISAGREE   STRONGLY DISAGREE

Teachers focus their professional development on the learning needs of their students.

STRONGLY AGREE   AGREE   NO OPINION   DISAGREE   STRONGLY DISAGREE

Professional development involves teachers working in teams to improve teaching and student learning.

STRONGLY AGREE   AGREE   NO OPINION   DISAGREE   STRONGLY DISAGREE

The majority of teacher professional development occurs at school.

STRONGLY AGREE   AGREE   NO OPINION   DISAGREE   STRONGLY DISAGREE

Teachers meet multiple times per week in teams to learn, reflect, and extend teaching and student learning.

STRONGLY AGREE   AGREE   NO OPINION   DISAGREE   STRONGLY DISAGREE

Decades of practice in professional learning demonstrated little long-term impact on teaching or student learning. Past professional development practices focused on building educators' expertise through workshops outside schools or conferences that individuals attended and then sometimes informally conveyed information about to colleagues. Practitioners and researchers recently have begun to examine professional learning practices to find common features that show results — long-lasting changes in teacher practices and improved student achievement.

An emerging consensus suggests that professional development that has the highest impact focuses directly on teachers' instructional content and material, takes place in their own schools and classrooms, includes coaching and ongoing feedback, and seeks to involve all teachers so that the learning is schoolwide rather than developing each individual's capacity independently (Miles, Odden, Fermanich, & Archibald, 2005, p. 9).

Until the last decade, teachers viewed professional

"For more than two decades, research has shown that teachers who experience frequent, rich learning opportunities have in turn been helped to teach in more ambitious and effective ways. Yet few teachers gain access to such intensive professional learning opportunities. More typically, teachers experience professional development as episodic, superficial, and disconnected from their own teaching interests or recurring problems of practice. This prevailing pattern — a few rich opportunities, many disappointing ones — speaks both to the promise and to the limitations of professional development, as it is typically organized. An important part of this enduring story centers on the schools and districts where teachers work and whether they are positioned well to foster professional learning opportunities that enhance the quality of teaching and learning."

— *Little, 2006, p. 1*

development as a matter of personal preference. Districts responded with a menu of workshops. No research has produced evidence that this approach is effective or that it produces changes in teaching behavior or results for students. In too many school systems, however, the catalogue-driven model of professional development still is the only kind of professional learning available. While educators do need opportunities to learn outside the school to meet the needs of those at different career stages and for individual preferences, outside professional development cannot be the only learning educators experience.

The core of effective professional learning is collaboration. As Dennis Sparks, NSDC's emeritus executive director, said: "If every student is to have a competent teacher, then virtually all their teachers must be learning virtually all the time. While that learning will occasionally happen in workshops and courses, most of it will occur as teachers plan lessons together, examine their students' work to find ways to improve it, observe one another teach, and plan improvements based on various data. Those of us concerned about teacher expertise must take leadership in designing such a system for learning" (Sparks, 1998, p. 2).

THE CASE FOR COLLABORATION

Collaborative professional learning is a form of professional development in which teachers work together to improve teaching and learning. "The term 'professional learning community' defines itself," says Melanie Morrissey (2000). "A school that operates as such engages the entire group of professionals in coming together for learning within a supportive, self-created community. Teacher and administrator learning is more complex, deeper, and more fruitful in a social setting, where the participants can interact, test their ideas, challenge their inferences and interpretations, and process new information with each other" (pp. 3-4).

Collaborative professional learning engages teachers in job-embedded, results-driven, and standards-based learning. NSDC's Standards for Staff Development (2001) advocate for professional learning that organizes teachers in learning communities whose goals align with those of the school and district. **Tool 2.2** includes the rationale for NSDC's Learning Communities standard. This rationale is a brief synthesis of the research and can help staff members understand the value of collaboration.

Judith Warren Little's research contributes some of the earliest and most definitive findings about the benefits of teachers learning together. She studied teachers as they worked together and found that regular, authentic, joint work focused on explicit goals for student learning "pays off richly in the form of higher-quality solutions to instructional problems, increased teacher confidence, and, not surprisingly, remarkable gains in student achievement" (Schmoker, 2005, 178).

If professional development occurs only after school hours or in the summer, districts are unlikely to have educators who spend 25% of their work time on learning.

Collaboration among educators builds shared responsibility and improves student learning. "Schools where teachers focus on student work, interact with colleagues to plan how to improve their teaching, and continuously bring new skills and knowledge to bear on their practice are also schools that produce the best results for students" (National Education Association Foundation for the Improvement of Education, 2000, p. 1).

Fred Newmann and Gary Wehlage (1995) identified common factors in schools that achieved disproportionately higher student performance in math, science, and social studies. These schools had staff members who formed learning communities, focused their attention on student work and assessment, and changed their instructional practices to improve their results with students. Common goals, consistent messages about learning objectives and methods, and collective responsibility, say Newmann and Wehlage, increase teacher efficacy. In addition, they believe that collaborative activity increases teachers' technical competence and collective responsibility.

> Collaborative professional learning engages teachers in teams that work together over time to improve teaching and learning. This approach has several attributes that distinguish it from other forms of professional learning.

"Collaborative activity can enhance teachers' technical competence. As teachers work with students from increasingly diverse social backgrounds, and as the curriculum begins to demand more intellectual rigor, teachers require information, technical expertise, and social-emotional support far beyond the resources they can muster as individuals working alone. When teachers collaborate productively, they participate in reflective dialogue to learn more about professional issues; they observe and react to one another's teaching, curriculum, and assessment practices; and they engage in joint planning and curriculum development. By enriching teachers' technical and social resources, collaboration can make teaching more effective.

"[C]learly shared purpose and collaboration contribute to collective responsibility: One's colleagues share responsibility for the quality of all students' achievement. This norm helps to sustain each teacher's commitment. A culture of collective responsibility puts more peer pressure and accountability on staff who may not have carried their fair share, but it can also ease the burden on teachers who have worked hard in isolation but who felt unable to help some students. In short,

professional community within the teaching staff sharpens the educational focus and enhances the technical and social support that teachers need to be successful" (Newmann & Wehlage, 1995, p. 31).

ATTRIBUTES OF COLLABORATIVE LEARNING

Collaborative professional learning engages teachers in teams that work together over time to improve teaching and learning. This approach has several attributes that distinguish it from other forms of professional learning.

Shirley Hord and a team of SEDL researchers reviewed the literature on professional communities and studied professional learning communities in 22 schools. As a result of their research, they identified five themes that served as the characteristics of teachers learning together in collaborative teams:

- Supportive and shared leadership requires collegial and facilitative participation of the principal, who shares leadership — and thus, power and authority — by inviting staff input and action in decision making.

- Shared values and vision include an unwavering commitment to student learning that is consistently articulated and referenced in the staff's work.

- Collective learning and application of learning requires that school staff at all levels are engaged in processes that collectively seek new knowledge among staff and application of the learning to solutions that address students' needs.

- Supportive conditions include physical and human capacities that encourage and sustain a collegial atmosphere and collective learning.

- Shared practice involves the review of a teacher's behavior by colleagues and includes feedback and assistance to support individual and community improvement (Hord, 2004, p. 7).

These themes describe the practices that prevail in schools in which teachers engage in genuine professional learning teams with colleagues.

Tool 2.1 can help educators understand the attributes of collaborative professional learning by having them work through an inquiry-based activity. This tool helps educators picture how collaborative professional learning might look in their school. Teams, of course, have the freedom to modify the concept of collaborative professional learning, provided the elements of NSDC's definition are evident in their work. Without those elements, collaboration will deviate from the research-supported practice and may fail to produce results for either educators or students.

CREATING COLLABORATION

Because collaboration is distinctively different from more traditional forms of professional learning such as workshops, courses, and training sessions, schools and districts should recognize that professional learning communities themselves are not the reform initiative, but rather are "the supporting structure for schools to continuously transform themselves though their own internal capacity" (Morrissey, p. 10). Some, however, view creating professional learning communities as their end goal rather than the means to the goal of improving student learning. Distinguishing the difference is essential to understanding the concept of collaborative professional learning.

Many educators have heard the term and even practice some attributes of the concept. Too often, though, their collaboration sessions resemble management or business meetings rather than genuine communities of practice. Developing a common understanding is the first step toward ensuring that collaboration among educators produces results for students.

This resource guide assists schools and teachers in linking professional learning to teachers' routine work by recognizing that collaborating about curriculum, assessment, instruction, and student learning is a legitimate form of professional development. Teachers will find that they more easily, quickly, and satisfactorily meet the requirement for 100 hours of professional development because the work that they have traditionally done in isolation is done with the added value of their colleagues' thinking. When teachers work collaboratively on their routine work and reflect on and continuously improve their practice, they will be driven less by the desire to earn professional development credits and more by the satisfaction of seeing the results of their learning.

Collaborative professional learning, according to Mike Schmoker, is "the best, least expensive, most professionally rewarding way to improve schools" (Schmoker, 2005, p. 137). It is the practice of educators working together to solve problems, and design and refine instruction, curriculum, assessments, and interventions for student learning. Collaborative professional learning uses practices that have long been successful in business and industry, such as quality circles, to bring teachers together within their school to co-construct, share, and distribute knowledge about teaching and learning throughout the school.

> Collaborative professional learning uses practices that have long been successful in business and industry.

A REWARDING WAY OF WORKING

Teachers who have committed to work in communities of learners report that getting started requires an investment of time and effort, but the rewards are significant. They say that their work is more satisfying, that they save time because they are sharing responsibility with peers, that their work is more focused, and that they would not return to the way they previously worked on their own. Schools in which teachers work in collaborative teams make steady progress toward improvement goals, have a clear focus, share goals, and produce results.

Collaborative professional learning will look different in large and small schools. In large schools, there are likely to be more and perhaps bigger teams. Teachers are more likely to serve on more than one collaborative team. The role of the principal, teacher leaders, and/or supervisors in coordinating and supporting the teams will be greater. Communication between and among teams will be more challenging and require more concerted effort. Creating a sense of community may be more challenging in a larger school where teachers do not work as closely together, although this is not necessarily a factor related to size, but is more closely connected to the culture within a school.

In smaller schools, teachers may serve on cross-level teams or interdisciplinary teams. Because teachers know each other better in smaller schools, teams are likely to become more productive more quickly. The principal may be able to be a member of all the teams in a smaller school. Certainly communication between and among teams will be easier. Creating a supportive culture may be easier because staff members are more likely to have a sense of community in a smaller school. Regardless of the size of the school, however, the process for creating teams is the same. The type of work teams do remains the same. The difference is the focus on multiple grades, courses, or core content areas rather than a single one.

DOING MORE TOGETHER

A recent study reported that a large percentage of teachers say they experience professional development, yet that the professional development they receive is not connected to their content and is not useful (Darling-Hammond, Wei, Andree, Richardson, & Orphanos,

VIDEO RESOURCES

These resources help educators see collaborative professional learning in action:

- NSDC's definition of professional development .
  www.nsdc.org/standfor/definition.cfm

- Critical friends groups from the Annenberg Institute for School Reform.
  www.annenberginstitute.org

- Designing and evaluating professional development for increased student learning from the School Improvement Network.
  www.schoolimprovement.com

- Let's talk about PLCs: Getting started (three parts) from Solution Tree.
  www.solution-tree.com

- Looking at student work: A window into the classroom from the Annenberg Institute for School Reform.
  www.annenberginstitute.org

- Looking at teacher work: Standards in practice
  www.collaborativecommunications.com

- Schools that learn: High standards for teacher and principal performance
  www.collaborativecommunications.com

- Whole-faculty study groups: Collaboration targeting student learning from the School Improvement Network.
  www.schoolimprovement.com

2009). With increased accountability, educators' resolve to ensure that every student experiences effective teaching every day requires that the balance of professional learning shift from external to internal learning and

REFLECTIONS

1. How could we benefit from collaborative professional learning?

2. What barriers appear to stand in the way of our implementing collaborative professional learning?

3. What aspects of collaborative professional learning are we already implementing? What aspects need more attention?

4. What is one action we can take to strengthen our practice of collaborative professional learning and its results?

5. What attitudes and understanding, or lack of, do we need to address to begin collaborative professional learning?

from the traditional to a reformed approach.

While both external and traditional professional learning are needed to infuse new ideas and practices into schools and classrooms, the real transformation in teacher learning happens at the school and classroom level. Implementing collaborative professional learning that embeds continuous improvement at the school and classroom level means that all students benefit from educator learning, not just some.

REFERENCES

Darling-Hammond, L., Wei, R., Andree, A., Richardson, N., & Orphanos, S. (2009). *Professional learning in the learning profession: A status report on teacher development in the United States and abroad.* Oxford, OH: NSDC.

Hord, S. (Ed.). (2004). *Learning together, leading together: Changing schools through professional learning communities.* New York: Teachers College Press.

Little, J.W. (2006). *Professional community and professional development in the learning-centered school.* Washington, DC: NEA.

Miles, K.H., Odden, A., Fermanich, M., &

Archibald, S. (2005). *Inside the black box: School district spending on professional development in education.* Washington, DC: The Finance Project.

Morrissey, M. (2000). *Professional learning communities: An ongoing exploration.* Austin, TX: SEDL.

The National Education Association Foundation. (n.d.) *Engaging public support for teachers' professional development.* Available at www.neafoundation. org/publications/engaging.htm#case.

National Staff Development Council. (2001). *NSDC's standards for staff development.* Oxford, OH: Author.

Newmann, F. & Wehlage, G. (1995). *Successful school restructuring.* Madison, WI: Center on Organization and Restructuring of Schools.

Schmoker, M. (2005). Here and now: Improving teaching and learning. In R. DuFour, R. Eaker, & R. DuFour (Eds.), *On common ground: The power of professional learning communities.* Bloomington, IN: Solution Tree.

Sparks, D. (1998, April). Teacher expertise linked to student learning. *Results, 2.*

TOOL INDEX

TOOL	TITLE	
2.1	Team learning scenario task	Tool 2.1 helps faculty members develop an understanding of the concept of collaborative professional learning and identify the characteristics that distinguish it from other forms of professional learning.
2.2	Learning Communities standard	Tool 2.2 is useful to deepen staff understanding of the attributes of an effective learning community focused on improving teaching and student learning.
2.3	Collaborative learning: Fears and hopes	Tool 2.3 engages school faculty in examining the potential barriers and benefits of collaborative professional learning.
2.4	Assessment of current reality of professional development	Tool 2.4 helps faculty examine where they are in relationship to the shift in professional learning and engages them in discussion to deepen their understanding of collaborative professional learning.
2.5	The best staff development is in the workplace, not in a workshop	Tool 2.5 provides a rationale for making the shift to school-based, collaborative professional learning.
2.6	A community of learners: One school's journey — two viewpoints	Tool 2.6 provides two perspectives on collaborative professional learning, a teacher's and a principal's.

PART 2

Setting

the

stage

Chapter 3

A CULTURE
of collaboration

WHERE ARE WE NOW?

Our school community believes that the school's culture affects educators' willingness to be continuous learners.

STRONGLY AGREE   AGREE   NO OPINION   DISAGREE   STRONGLY DISAGREE

Attaining our learning goals for students depends on staff's ability to work together well as colleagues.

STRONGLY AGREE   AGREE   NO OPINION   DISAGREE   STRONGLY DISAGREE

A high level of trust exists between teachers and administrators in our school and district.

STRONGLY AGREE   AGREE   NO OPINION   DISAGREE   STRONGLY DISAGREE

A primary outcome of our professional development is to cultivate in-house expertise in instruction, curriculum, and assessment.

STRONGLY AGREE   AGREE   NO OPINION   DISAGREE   STRONGLY DISAGREE

Educators in our school challenge each other to accept no excuses for low student achievement.

STRONGLY AGREE   AGREE   NO OPINION   DISAGREE   STRONGLY DISAGREE

The bottom line is this: *We can do more together than any one of us can do alone.* When teachers work together, they can solve complex problems of practice. They share their expertise so that all students benefit from what each teacher knows. When teachers come together in this way, they can bring about unstoppable change.

"There is no power greater than a community discovering what it cares about," asserts Margaret Wheatley (2002, p. 145). Teachers change when they have opportunities to collaborate and uncover those mutual interests. The school's culture and climate change as teachers change. And school culture affects teachers' attitudes toward collaboration. Culture and collaboration are inextricably intertwined.

What is school culture? It's more than morale. School culture can be defined as the historically transmitted patterns of meaning that include the norms, values, beliefs, ceremonies, rituals, traditions, and myths understood, in varying degrees, by members of the school community. This system of meaning often shapes what people think and how they act.

"My colleagues and I were excited. We realized that we had the power to effect change by working collaboratively … and we realized we could learn more from each other than we could from any one-day workshop. The sharing of craft knowledge fostered an excitement for professional learning. Other teachers from the district, as well as other school communities, visited our classrooms, extending our learning community outside our own school's walls."

— Beth Warren, former teacher, in
*A Community of Learners: One School's
Journey — Two Viewpoints*

NSDC's Standards for Staff Development include context standards as one of the three major categories (context, process, and content), signaling that organizational culture, support, leadership, and resources are essential for creating effective, job-embedded professional learning within a school or district (**Figure 3.1**). In other words, a strong collaborative culture that values

Figure 3.1 NSDC'S STANDARDS FOR STAFF DEVELOPMENT

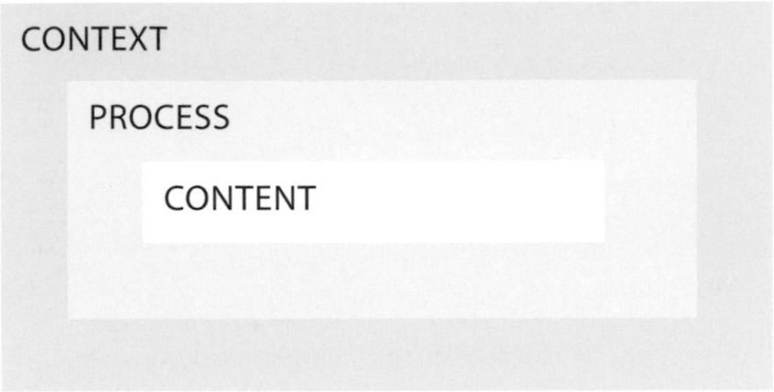

CONTEXT

PROCESS

CONTENT

continuous improvement, honors teacher and administrator expertise, expects ongoing learning about teaching, and invites faculty innovation is an essential element of a high-performing school.

WHAT IS CULTURE?

Louise Stoll, a leading British researcher, defined school culture as "how things are done around here" (1999). School culture manifests itself in customs, routines, rituals, symbols, stories, expectations, and language — culture's "artifacts." **Table 3.1** outlines Stoll's indicators of school culture.

Cultural patterns are powerful. They shape and mold the way people think, act, feel, and more importantly, they affect individuals' performances.

WHY CULTURE MATTERS

The importance of school culture was recognized as early as the 1930s (Jerald, 2006), but the link between school culture and educational outcomes was not forged until the 1970s. Researchers have found that healthy and sound school cultures correlate strongly with increased student achievement and motivation, and with teacher productivity and satisfaction (Deal & Peterson, 2009). Marzano's meta-analysis (2003) of school factors that lead to high levels of student achievement and learning describes the need for professionalism and collegiality. And in a study of thousands of teachers from 134 randomly selected schools, Craig Jerald (2006)

asked teachers to describe their school culture and sorted the results according to whether schools were considered high- or low-performing. The results indicate:

HIGH-PERFORMING SCHOOLS FOCUSED ON:
- Hunger for improvement;
- Raising capability — helping people learn;
- The value added;
- Promoting excellence — pushing the boundaries of achievement;
- Making sacrifices to put pupils first.

LOW-PERFORMING SCHOOLS FOCUSED ON:
- Warmth, humor, repartee;
- Recognizing personal circumstances, making allowances — "it's the effort that counts";
- Creating a pleasant and collegial working environment.

Studies of school culture have found that positive school culture was a prime contributor to student academic success, could determine whether improvement efforts withered or succeeded, and cultivated school effectiveness and productivity (Deal & Peterson, 1999).

> **Cultural patterns are powerful. They shape and mold the way people think, act, feel, and more importantly, they affect individuals' performances.**

In an extensive study of literacy teachers' success and the working conditions of the schools in which they taught, Judith Langer discovered students who outperformed their peers attended schools that nurtured a professional climate for teachers.

THE FACTORS THAT EMERGED ACROSS ALL THE SCHOOLS STUDIED INCLUDE:
- A shared vision for student achievement and a plan to get there;
- Teacher participation in a variety of professional

communities in and outside of the school and valuing their commitment to the profession of teaching;

- Structured improvement activities that offered teachers a sense of agency;
- Caring attitude that extends to colleagues and students; and
- Deep respect for lifelong learning (Langer, 2001, 2002).

ELEMENTS OF A COLLABORATIVE CULTURE

A collaborative culture needs to be distinguished from a congenial environment. Most school staff care about and comfort one another. Educators have incredible capacity to attend to personal events or challenges: a baby's birth, a wedding, or the need for sick days due to catastrophic illness. Those are the characteristics of a congenial environment. To succeed, a school must move beyond congeniality into genuine collegiality.

School cultures characterized by collegiality and professionalism rather than congeniality promote teacher conversations about their work (Fullan & Hargreaves, 1996). A collegial school staff works together with a tight focus on learning, high-quality teaching, student success, and overcoming barriers — the traits that distinguish a good school from a great one.

Judith Warren Little's early work, conducted by listening to conversations in the teachers' lounge, identified four norms that support changes in classroom instruction (Little, 1981, pp. 10-11) leading to high-performing cultures:

- **"Teachers engage in frequent, continuous, and increasingly concrete and precise *talk* about teaching *practice*."** These conversations result in a shared language among teachers. A shared language enables teachers to go beyond the surface and explore the complexities of high-quality instruction. "The concreteness, precision, and coherence of the

SUCCESS STRATEGIES

In a study of schools that received the U.S. Department of Education Model Professional Development Program Award in 1997 and 1998, researchers found striking similarities among the schools that used professional development as the means to improve student learning. The research team offered the following recommendations:

- Use clear, agreed-upon student achievement goals to focus and shape student learning;
- Provide an expanded array of professional development opportunities;
- Embed ongoing informal learning into the school culture;
- Build a highly collaborative school environment where working together to solve problems and learning from each other become the cultural norm;
- Find and use the time to allow teacher learning to happen; and
- Keep checking a broad range of student performance data (WestEd, 2000, p. 12).

shared language" leads to high-quality experimentation with new instructional practices and more rigorous collegial interaction, according to Little.

- **"Teachers and administrators frequently *observe* each other teaching and provide each other with useful … evaluations of their teaching."** Most people experience a gap between knowing and doing. The best feedback is based on actual observation of classroom practice that focuses on common terminology and critical attributes of practice. While this kind of collegial interaction can be sen-

Table 3.1 STOLL'S SCHOOL CULTURE INDICATORS

Aspects of school culture	Visible evidence
Celebrations	How staff and student successes and achievements are recognized and celebrated.
Stories	How the school community talks about the school itself — its history and myths; whose stories are told and whose are overlooked; stories the community and the school tell about the school.
Shared sayings	The language the school uses to talk about itself, e.g. "We're a community school."
Taboos	What is not allowed within the school, explicitly and implicitly, from types of behavior to how certain groups or people are treated.
Ways of rewarding	Intrinsic or extrinsic rewards to staff and students; acknowledgements.
Rituals	How common events are run and what is emphasized at them: Athletic achievement? Discipline? Academic achievement? Community contributions?
Communications	How messages, positive and negative, are delivered to the school or wider community; the channels, levels of, and pathways for communication within the school.
Behaviors	How students and staff treat each other; the level of respect, trust, collaboration, and sharing evident; how guests are treated.
Rites of exit and entry	How new staff members are inducted; how farewells for staff and students are conducted; how new students and new parents are welcomed.
Events	The focus of significant annual events like awards, school plays, field day, homecoming, prom, etc.

Source: **Stoll, L. (1999).** School culture: Black hole or fertile garden for school improvement. In J. Prosser (Ed.), *School culture.* British Educational Management Series. London: Sage Publications.

sitive, it remains a powerful strategy for building collaboration skills.

- **"Teachers and administrators *plan, design, research, evaluate, and prepare teaching materials together.*"** Before new practices or materials are actually used in the classroom, most teachers spend time preparing. When teachers and administrators work together, their collaboration reinforces the idea that joint work takes less time, builds a com-

mon understanding of the new approach, and supports each person in reaching a high-quality level in using new practices.

- **"Teachers and administrators teach each other the practice of teaching."** This norm goes beyond creating formal mentor or lead teacher positions to allowing teachers to share practices that help students succeed. Teaching one another is the essence of job-embedded professional learning. When small learning teams work on developing new practices, review student work, and solve problems together, they create a collaborative culture that benefits both adults and students.

School and district cultures encourage or discourage collaboration. "Schools' organizational conditions function either as a centripetal force pulling teachers to pursue common purpose or as a *centrifugal* force pushing teachers to pursue individual purpose" (Rosenholtz, 1991, p. 63).

BUILDING A COLLABORATIVE CULTURE

Teachers, students, parents, staff, and the principal collaborate to create a vision for a healthy school culture. The principal's role in changing school culture is to act with care and concern for others, work to develop shared visions of what the school should be, and work on team building (Stolp, 1994).

Creating the conditions that support teacher collaborative learning also means helping teachers build trust, relationships, and voice. Jody Westbrook and Shirley Hord describe conditions necessary for professional learning communities that emerged from their study of different school settings (2000). They found "significant foundational factors" — the presence of which contributed to professional learning community success, and the absence of which often presaged difficulty or failure in professional learning community implementation:

Trust. High levels of trust among teachers, between teachers and administrators, between campus and district-level personnel, and between school personnel and co-developers promote risk taking, honest communication, and deep commitments to school initiatives, including professional learning communities. The absence of trust distracts personnel from instructional issues to focus on conflicts of personality and practice. Conscious efforts to build trust characterize many efforts to create professional learning communities.

A listening atmosphere. Schools in which leaders solicit and use teachers' insights and input move more easily into — or increase their practice of —the learning community characteristics of shared leadership and collective learning. Administrators who act without teacher input tend toward autocratic leadership styles and have staffs who feel their knowledge is not honored and their suggestions not welcomed. In these schools, staffs tend to resist top-down directives, including collaborating.

Student-centered. Although one might expect any school to focus on students, visitors to a cross section of the nation's schools will quickly find many ways teachers and administrators can be distracted from student learning and well-being. Administrators and teachers alike can be consumed by issues such as test scores and their implications for funding, status, and consequences within a district; staff turnover and political concerns; personality clashes; and equity issues within and between schools.

Schools where personnel ask aloud and frequently of programs, practices, and initiatives, "Is it better for kids?" more easily and deeply take on collaboration and more easily tailor how that looks to their school's particular needs and culture.

Concern about add-on programs. The plethora of new initiatives, innovations, projects, and reform efforts, combined with hefty demands of teaching, have led many school personnel to a sense of "so much to do, so little time."

Rather than being a sign of resistance, teachers' questions about additional responsibilities and time required for collaborative learning teams reveal a healthy skepticism about poorly planned or implemented reform efforts.

When these concerns are addressed openly and completely, teachers and administrators are able to more fully commit to creating a professional learning community at their school (Westbrook & Hord, 2000, pp. 2-4).

FIRST STEPS

Does teacher collaboration create a collegial culture or does a positive, professional culture inspire, promote, and sustain teacher collaboration? Which comes first has no definitive answer. School cultures increase teachers' willingness to engage in collaborative professional learning, and teachers' willingness to collaborate improves school culture. The reciprocal relationship between culture and collaboration sometimes makes it difficult to determine whether to begin working toward change by trying first to establish a culture that supports teacher interdependence or to begin with creating communities of learners.

While both options have merit, a good place to begin is by accepting existing conditions and recognizing that, regardless of where a school starts, both culture and willingness to work together will be positively impacted.

Steps toward collaboration can be quickly subdued by a school culture that does not value collegiality. Cultural forces are powerful and subtly determine what is done — or not done — within the school.

The principal plays a critical role, developing and sustaining trust within the building and influencing the culture. School leaders can act to:

Build trust

Trust among school community members can make or break efforts to reform classroom practices, implement curriculum, or improve student performance (Bryk & Schneider, 2003). Tony Bryk and Barbara Schneider's finding suggests that the level of trust, respect, and collegial interaction among school staff may be more critical than structural changes typically focused on during reform efforts.

Trust is crucial because many change efforts inherently involve risk. "When school professionals trust one another and sense support from parents, they feel safe to experiment with new practices" (Bryk & Schneider, 2003, p.43).

Assess the current culture

The first step in developing a school culture that supports continuous, job-embedded professional learning is to assess the current culture. Determining how to assess school culture is a decision that is best made collaboratively by the principal and teacher leadership team. Before selecting a tool to use, both the principal and teacher leaders will want to study options, weigh the pros and cons of each, and select one that will be informative, not overwhelming.

The tools included for this chapter on the CD are examples of ways to assess school culture. If the school has not conducted a formal culture audit, a better choice may be a simpler tool.

As the school develops a culture of openness and inquiry, other tools may be used. Regardless of the tool or process, regularly assessing school culture ensures that actions to strengthen the culture are data-driven and focused on areas of need.

Reinforce the positive

The next step is to transform the culture by "reinforcing positive aspects and working to transform negative aspects" (Peterson, 2002, p. 14). By first reading and assessing the culture, school leaders — both administrators and teachers — know what behaviors and values to reinforce and which to transform. In their work on school culture, Deal and Peterson (1999, p. 127-128) suggest the following strategies for overcoming a negative cultures:

1. Confront negativity head-on; give people a chance to vent publicly.

2. Shield and support positive cultural elements and staff.

3. Focus energy on recruiting, selecting, and retaining effective, positive staff members.

4. Celebrate the positive and the possible.

5. Focus consciously and directly on eradicating negatives and rebuilding around positive norms and beliefs.

6. Develop new stories of success, renewal, and accomplishment.

7. Help those who might succeed and thrive in a new district make the move to a new school.

Similarly, a principal can develop collaborative norms and practices within a school by:

1. **Announcing and describing** norms and practices intended to build collaboration among faculty. Take any opportunity to discuss, focus, and reinforce the importance of these practices, particularly at meaningful occasions such as the first staff meeting of the year, to clearly signal to staff the importance of collegial practice to the school's core work. These messages must be reinforced frequently and in a variety of situations "to confirm and specify the desired interactions among teachers" (Little, 1981, p. 13).

2. **Modeling or enacting** the desired behavior. The principal, as well as other staff members, can model. The principal should demonstrate his/her own use of collaborative skills, conduct classroom walk-throughs that reinforce collaboration, transform staff meetings into time for collegial interaction, and provide time for teachers to work together.

3. **Sanctioning** the announced and modeled behavior. Endorse and approve collaboration and collegiality. Although principals typically don't have cash to provide incentives, they can sanction by offering "released time, by visible and public praise

for collegial or experimental efforts, by tolerating and absorbing inevitable failures encountered in experimentation" (Little, 1981, p. 13).

4. **Defending** the norms. Even though collegial norms are positive and powerful, the established school culture and forces outside the school, such as the district and parents, will create inevitable push-back. The principal will need strength of conviction to stand up to these countermovements. Judith Warren Little (1981) suggests identifying common interests rather than focusing on opposing positions.

REPLACING THE PAST

Past professional development practices have focused on building the expertise of individual educators outside schools rather than the expertise of teams within schools. Replacing that practice with the research-supported practice of developing collaborative learning teams that focus on professional learning and student success improves schools' bottom line — student achievement.

Establishing conditions that support collaborative professional learning is challenging. Yet when staff members begin to collaborate, they interact about teaching and learning since that is their common interest and develop trust and respect for one another. They simultaneously increase the transparency of their work and create interdependence. The relationship between creating teams and creating a collaborative culture is reciprocal. Act on one, and the other responds.

REFERENCES

Bryk, A. & Schneider, B. (2003, March). Trust in schools: A core resource for school reform. *Educational Leadership, 60*(6), 40-45.

Deal, T. & Peterson, K. (1999). *Shaping school culture: The heart of leadership.* San Francisco: Jossey-Bass.

REFLECTIONS

1. Some say that trust is more important than structural changes to the success of collaborative professional learning. Do you agree? Why?

2. What examples or experiences do you have that support the argument that a positive, collegial culture leads to higher levels of student achievement?

3. Do you believe that school culture can be shaped? If so, why?

4. Terrence Deal and Kent Peterson propose that both principals and teacher leaders attack negativity within the culture. What support do leaders need to do so?

5. What role do principals and teacher leaders play in developing a collaborative culture within a school? How do they know if they are successful?

Deal, T. & Peterson, K. (2009). *Shaping school culture: Pitfalls, paradoxes, and promises.* San Francisco: Jossey Bass.

Fullan, M. & Hargreaves, A. (1996). *What's worth fighting for in your school?* New York: Teachers College Press.

Jerald, C. (2006, December). *School culture: "The hidden curriculum."* Washington, DC: The Center for Comprehensive School Reform and Improvement. Available at www.centerforcsri.org/files/Center_IB_Dec06_C.pdf.

Langer, J. (2001). Beating the odds: Teaching middle school and high school students to read and write well. *American Educational Research Journal, 38*(4), 837-880.

Langer, J. (2002). *Effective literacy instruction: Building successful reading and writing programs.* Urbana, IL: National Council of Teachers of English.

Little, J.W. (1981, January). *School success and staff development: The role of staff development in urban desegregated schools.* Boulder, CO: Center for Action Research.

Marzano, R. (2003). *What works in schools: Translating research into action.* Alexandria, VA: ASCD.

Peterson, K.D. (2002, Summer). Positive or negative. *Journal of Staff Development, 23*(3), 10-15.

Rosenholtz, S. (1991). *Teachers' workplace: The social organization of schools.* New York: Teachers College Press.

Stoll, L. (1999). School culture: Black hole or fertile garden for school improvement. In J. Prosser (Ed.), *School culture.* British Educational Management Series. London: Sage Publications.

Stolp, S. (1994). *Leadership for school culture.* East Lansing, MI: National Center for Research on Teacher Learning.

Westbrook, J. & Hord, S. (2000). Introduction. In R. Chapman, R. Hinson, K. Hipp, C. Jacoby, J. Huffman, A. Pankake, B. Sattes, J. Thomas, & J. Westbrook, *Multiple mirrors: Reflections on the creation of professional learning communities.* Austin, TX: SEDL.

WestEd. (2000). *Teachers who learn, kids who achieve.* San Francisco: Author.

Wheatley, M. (2002). *Turning to one another: Simple conversations to restore hope to the future.* San Francisco: Berrett-Koehler.

TOOL INDEX

TOOL	TITLE	USE
3.1	Culture is …	Tool 3.1 describes a conversation that helps explain how the organization's culture is viewed by staff members.
3.2	Learning about your school's culture	Tool 3.2 is a survey that assesses school culture based on the 12 norms of a healthy school identified by Jon Saphier and Matthew King.
3.3	An audit of the culture starts with two handy tools	Tool 3.3 is a multistep approach to assessing current culture.
3.4	Positive or negative	Tool 3.4 examines the characteristics of positive and negative school culture. This article also describes methods for assessing current culture.
3.5	Change agent	Tool 3.5 describes the impact of a positive school culture on student achievement.
3.6	Collaboration is the key to unlocking potential	Tool 3.6 describes five tasks the principal needs to do to create a culture that expects and supports adult learning within the school.
3.7	'Collaboration lite' puts student achievement on a starvation diet	Tool 3.7 defines the characteristics of high-powered, high-quality professional collaboration.
3.8	Q & A: Leadership can quickly turn around school culture	Tool 3.8 describes steps the principal can take to create a positive school culture that supports learning for students and adults.
3.9	Trust is the on-ramp to building collaboration and collegiality	Tool 3.9 addresses the importance of trust and describes strategies for the principal to build trust.
3.10	Student learning grows in professional cultures	Tool 3.10 provides a variety of resources and tools designed to assess and shape a school culture that focuses on improved student learning.
3.11	Pull out negativity by its roots	Tool 3.11 identifies values that offset countervailing attitudes and beliefs common in some schools.
3.12	A new role: Cultural architect	Tool 3.12 proposes ways to involve teachers in developing a positive culture within a school.
3.13	Build the infrastructure first	Tool 3.13 describes actions the principal can take to ensure that teachers know how to collaborate and focus on student learning.

Chapter 4

PROMOTING
change

WHERE ARE WE NOW?

Teachers in our school embrace change.

STRONGLY AGREE   AGREE   NO OPINION   DISAGREE   STRONGLY DISAGREE

We have a history of successful change efforts to draw from as we move to collaborative professional learning.

STRONGLY AGREE   AGREE   NO OPINION   DISAGREE   STRONGLY DISAGREE

The school leadership team members work closely together to implement collaborative professional learning teams.

STRONGLY AGREE   AGREE   NO OPINION   DISAGREE   STRONGLY DISAGREE

We address resistance to collaborative professional learning using thoughtful strategies that honor different perspectives.

STRONGLY AGREE   AGREE   NO OPINION   DISAGREE   STRONGLY DISAGREE

Resources are available to support the change to collaborative professional learning.

STRONGLY AGREE   AGREE   NO OPINION   DISAGREE   STRONGLY DISAGREE

Transformational change alters the way people think and act. It changes how they interact with one another and how they view their work. Working in a collaborative professional learning team is a transformational change.

Teachers who leave the isolation of their classrooms and solitary planning practices for group work and support begin to feel less as though collaborating is another assignment added to a stack, and collaboration instead becomes a way of working and increasing individuals' potential. These educators genuinely transform how they think about their work as professionals and seek peer support and expertise, as well as lending theirs whenever necessary. They discover that working together allows them to accomplish more than they ever imagined while working alone. Their work is more fulfilling, challenging, and rewarding. Their collective experiences give them new insights into shaping student interactions and learning opportunities in classrooms so that they also help students learn collaboration as an important life skill.

Yet change causes people to act in unexpected ways. Implementing collaborative professional learning among educators who have been independently responsible for their own classrooms requires thoughtful, intentional planning to address people's concerns about doing things differently. Research on educational change offers practical strategies to support people as they shift from more independent teaching practices to collaboration.

UNDERSTANDING CHANGE

Understanding how individuals experience change will help leaders planning new initiatives. Here are some basics about change:

People respond differently to change.

Some people pride themselves on perfecting their practices and worry that change will diminish their effectiveness. Those who for years have experienced real or perceived success find it difficult to entertain new ideas. They question the value of changing if what they currently do works as they imagine it should and they are competent at those practices.

Those leading new initiatives, on the other hand,

often are advocates who love change and pursue it. Change advocates often are frustrated by those slower to respond or who actively resist. Worrying about late adopters or resisters, however, does little to accelerate the speed of change.

Change can cause divisiveness.

The divisiveness that occurs in systems between those leading change and those who resist it can have a lasting impact on any innovation's effectiveness. Those who enthusiastically embrace an innovation often find their values conflicting with those who do not want to change. Those who resist change often feel undervalued by those who are promoting it.

Conflict is a natural part of change.

Conflict during change is natural. Sometimes the conflict is internal about one's own values and beliefs. Sometimes a disagreement is with others about data, procedures, or expectations, or over existing and new priorities. Without conflict, little really changes — a fundamentally scientific principle. Disequilibrium leads to the creation of a new equilibrium. Without disequilibrium, systems don't change. The same it true of schools and educators.

Change is a process.

Schools often introduce teachers to a new instructional strategy or curriculum in an hour or two after school or just before the school year begins, expecting that each educator will immediately and fully implement the learning. Not every educator can make such instant and dramatic changes after an awareness session. For some, change requires mulling over the new knowledge, acquiring needed skills, practicing, and receiving feedback.

Internalizing change often requires people to reshape their attitudes about their capabilities, role, and

ADAPTING TO CHANGE

Everett Rogers (2003) described how well people adapt to change. According to Rogers:

2.5% of people are **innovators**, cutting-edge pioneers who often embrace change.

13.5% are **early adopters** who venture into the innovation to try it and who influence those who follow.

34% are the **early majority**, cautious, thoughtful adapters who accept change more quickly then the late majority.

34% are the **late majority**, those who come to change late and only when there is evidence that the majority are engaged in the innovation.

16% are **laggards**, those who will accept change only when they experience pressure to do so and when it is clear that the innovation is the new way of doing business.

competence, as well as time to gather data about results (Hall & Hord, 2001).

Too many changes can derail all improvement efforts.

Some organizations implement multiple changes at once. Educators may want to make many changes knowing they have limited time with students and wanting to improve as much as possible. For example, a school might try to implement a new reading curriculum, new math curriculum, assessment for learning, and a focus on 21st-century skills at the same time.

Those implementing the new programs may find it difficult to manage so much new information simultaneously and may not see how the efforts are related. When changes are significant and those responsible don't connect the initiatives, the focus on all fronts can disrupt the potential for the success of any. Teachers will concentrate on implementing one strategy well, not intending any disservice to the other programs. As a result of trying to do too much, nothing gets done thoroughly, and the potential success of any improvement effort is minimized.

Organizations change only if the people in them change.

Research on change in education that remains as relevant today as when it was first done revealed that system changes occur not by adjusting structure or process, but only when people within the organization change (Hord, Rutherford, Huling-Austin, & Hall, 2005). For schools to alter their results, teachers and principals need to change. Teachers and principals will find it difficult to change if central office administrators

> Collaborative professional learning cannot be successful if the change occurs at the surface.

don't. This chain reaction means that any change must flow through the whole system.

Schools will not become collaborative learning environments unless the people working in them become collaborators. When teachers and principals adopt the innovation and fully implement the new practices, change will occur. As more people adopt the innovation, the culture of the school community will shift.

KEYS TO THE CHANGE PROCESS

Change takes place at different intensities. Dennis Sparks, NSDC's emeritus executive director, describes the alternatives of deep change or slow death. Drawing

from the work of Robert Quinn, author of *Deep Change: Discovering the Leader Within,* Sparks notes, "Deep change counteracts the naturally occurring forces of decline that operate in all organizations and dramatically increases the likelihood that improvements in teaching and learning are sustained rather than dissipated when a leader moves on or a project's funding ends. It occurs when organizations have compelling and ambitious visions for their collective future that require alterations in structures, roles, processes, and, most importantly, in the beliefs, understandings, and practices of the community members" (Sparks, 2009, p. 1).

Collaborative professional learning cannot be successful if the change occurs at the surface. Surface change such as altering the school schedule or having a staff training session on how to collaborate and what to do within collaborative time does not lead to different results. Surface changes are necessary, but insufficient. They may spark some actions for a short time, but are unlikely to alter how teachers think about their instruction and the quality of teaching.

Michael Fullan, a long-time expert in the field, writes in the *The New Meaning of Educational Change* (2007) that successful change requires two forces, pressure and support. Pressure is not the same as force, but is equated with purposefulness, intentionality, and clarity. Pressure for change includes stating the purpose of it; clarifying what is expected of those involved; setting precise timelines; holding people accountable; and identifying specific results. The vision for the change becomes embedded in practice by leaders sending these messages about the initiative multiple times using many different forms of communication. Pressure also includes monitoring implementation and results and providing ongoing, clear processes for addressing those less willing to change. (See sidebar on resistance.)

As changes are implemented, intermittent setbacks are a given. Setbacks always are part of an adjustment process. Things improve for a little while, then when the reality of the change sets in, things are worse for a while. The implementation dip hits.

Those who have monitored change will have seen firsthand that dips occur. The evidence is a drop in student scores, more frustrated teachers, and gaps in implementation. When scores drop and teachers are frustrated, they resort to past practices that are comfortable. When they do, students become confused, and the result is even lower scores, especially when assessments are based on the innovation. This cycle continues until the change fades into habit or a new change comes along, as new initiatives inevitably do.

Muscling through an implementation dip requires persistence and data. Leaders use data, not opinions, to search for areas that require attention. Data may show that practitioners need more training in a particular practice or a coach to demonstrate, debrief, and co-teach lessons. Strategies that help lift people out of the implementation dip include feedback and additional support, including peer visitations, problem-solving sessions, resources, or just an opportunity to talk about some of the challenges. Reaching the goal of real change requires that leaders acknowledge a dip, address concerns, refine implementation, and stay the course.

SUPPORTING CHANGE

Who leads the change and who is viewed as supporting it matter as much as who has been involved in shaping it. When more people are involved, more may be on board, yet numbers are a false pretense. Success depends more on the visible support that engages people in change, a deep understanding of the benefits to them, clear expectations, and clarity of results.

Leaders require support to implement and maintain change. Leaders need a number of opportunities to learn about the change and about the skills and behaviors needed to succeed. They need adequate resources,

including people, time, and equipment, or whatever the change requires. They need ongoing feedback and ruthless assessment of progress toward identified benchmarks and goals. Support for them also includes celebrations, encouragement, and troubleshooting when needed. Support means coaching, problem solving, sharing successes and challenges, tapping expertise within the school, and building the capacity of others. Most of all, support means allowing adequate time for change to occur, without too much time to allow any momentum to evaporate. Change is hard. People sometimes give up before it is achieved. Real change in education means everyone in a school is learning. As they learn, they see a few immediate rewards, but experience degrees of anxiety and concern.

> Success depends more on the visible support that engages people in change, a deep understanding of the benefits to them, clear expectations, and clarity of results.

Those leading school initiatives can draw on a body of research that a team at the University of Texas at Austin and SEDL developed more than 30 years ago to bring about change more successfully. The Concerns-Based Adoption Model (CBAM) provides insights into how educators respond to new initiatives. In studying how educators implement curriculum, the research team discovered that teachers move through seven distinct stages of concern about an innovation, from barely recognizable interest in the new effort to complete engagement.

When a principal or teacher leader responsible for implementing collaborative professional learning teams understands these stages and knows how to recognize the stage and what interventions to use to address the concerns expressed at each stage, he or she has the advantage of providing specific rather than general support. By truly understanding a person's concerns and responding appropriately, the change leader connects

RESISTANCE

Resistance is inevitable. Newton's third law of physics says that every action has an equal and opposite reaction. This law suggests several important concepts in thinking about resistance in change. First, resistance occurs when two forces are at work. Jim Knight (2009) cites the work of William Miller and Stephen Rollnick, who explored how resistance plays out in counseling and therapy. Miller and Rollnick confirm that resistance cannot occur with one person acting alone. Resistance requires two, the actor and the reactor. The laws of physics also suggest that any act will have a reaction. In addition, force is an important consideration. In flight, drag and thrust are at work. In human change efforts, pressure and support are at work, along with trust and relationships.

Resistance takes many forms. Rick Mauer, an organizational development specialist, says resistance occurs at three levels (1996).

Level one

Level one happens when people don't have enough information. Most people need data, graphics, pictures, and information that help them understand the change and the reason for it. Sometimes they disagree with the data, and additional information may not help. In these cases, the resistance is probably at a different level.

Level two

Level two resistance is emotionally driven and connected to identity. People resist because the change means they lose control, status, or identity. This kind of resistance is easy to address through open forums, where people can voice their concerns without being told to get over it. Leaders who don't want to hear complaints or criticism

personally with the person expressing the concern and minimizes resistance. For example, if a teacher says she doesn't understand how teaming with colleagues in her department will help her become a better teacher, a response detailing how students will benefit from teacher collaborative learning will not address her concerns. That teacher may feel that she was discounted or that she was not heard, and she may begin building resentment toward the change leader and build resistance to the change.

The stages of concern are listed in **Table 4.1** with strategies team members can use to respond to those who are concerned about collaborating in professional learning teams. Other tools for this chapter on the CD

include strategies for coaches and principals.

The value of knowing about a stage of concern is that those working to have the initiative succeed can listen to concerns and respond in a way that matches individual needs. For example, if a teacher expresses a management concern and a colleague responds with a Stage 4 Consequence intervention strategy, the concerned teacher's resistance may increase because he feels his issues were not heard or addressed. A formal stages of change questionnaire can help leaders assess what people are feeling and thinking about an initiative at various points during the change. The questionnaire, *Measuring Implementation in Schools: The Stages of Concern Questionnaire* (George, Hall, & Stiegelbauer, may find open forums difficult; however, the best tool for this stage is listening, acknowledging, and keeping relationships in the forefront. Keeping lines of communication and support open helps, too. If people see and feel support, they are less fearful about the implications of a change. Leaders can remember the WIIFM rule (what's in it for me) and speak frequently about how the change benefits the individual (see Personal Concern in **Table 4.1**).

Level three

According to Mauer, level three resistance targets the change leader or the organization. This form of resistance occurs because people distrust the organization's leader. Mauer says they may have past experience with the person or the organization that makes them wary. When those assigned to carry out change see the leader as untrustworthy or not credible, change is unlikely

to occur. The first necessary action is to build relational trust.

Leaders cannot ignore resistance and expect it to dissipate. Resistance requires attention and effort. If ignored, resistance can get out of control and derail change. Leaders, whether they are teacher leaders or administrators, demonstrate their commitment to any change by acting quickly and positively to address resistance.

Not all forms of resistance will be overcome easily. Some individuals' resistance can be overcome with trust, clarity of expectations, commitment to support individuals, and resources. For some, time and staying the course will make a difference. Sometimes reform, particularly deep change, leads to changes in personnel. Ultimately, commitment and willingness to support the change will determine whether change moves from a temporary to permanent state.

2006), has been revised and may help in schoolwide planning.

PLAN TO SUCCEED

Change is never easy, even for those who enjoy new challenges. Teachers whose practice has long been independent and isolated find collaboration particularly difficult. The rewards of collaboration may not come immediately and the work may seem to multiply rather than diminish.

To ensure success, leaders of collaboration plan carefully and thoughtfully to launch this new form of professional learning, design and implement comprehensive plans to move from a set of goals and a vision

to practice, monitor progress and provide results, refine their pathways as they go using data not hunches, and celebrate small successes along the way.

They invest in people, systems, and structures and recognize that what is worth doing well takes time, effort, and resources, along with commitment and courage.

REFERENCES

Fullan, M. (2007). *The new meaning of educational change* (4th ed.). New York: Teachers College Press.

George, A., Hall, G., & Stiegelbauer, S. (2006). *Measuring implementation in schools: The Stages of Con-*

REFLECTIONS

1. As a school, what is our experience with change? Thinking back over the last five years, what changes have we implemented successfully? Which changes have not gone well? What did we learn from these experiences that will help us as we change the way we work and learn together?

2. What forms of resistance seem to be most troublesome in our school? What are we doing to purposefully address resistance in positive and productive ways?

3. As we think about reflecting NSDC's definition of quality professional development in how we learn in our school, what strengths do we bring and what opportunities do we have for our students, our staff, and our community?

4. What do we want to remember as we move through our change work? If we do just one thing differently from past change processes, what will it be?

5. What is my personal response to changes in my professional work? How does my response differ from my colleagues'? What impact do these differences have on our ability to work together to implement new initiatives?

cern Questionnaire. Austin, TX: SEDL.

Hall, G. & Hord, S. (2001). *Implementing change: Patterns, principles, and potholes.* Boston: Allyn & Bacon.

Hord, S., Rutherford, W., Huling-Austin, L., & Hall, G. (2005). *Taking charge of change.* Austin, TX: SEDL.

Knight, J. (2009). What can we do about teacher resistance? *Phi Delta Kappan, 90*(7), 508-513.

Mauer, R. (1996). *Beyond the walls of resistance: Unconventional strategies that build support for change.* Austin, TX: Bard Press.

Rogers, E. (2003). *Diffusion of innovation.* New York: Free Press.

Sparks, D. (2009, March 9). Leaders choose "deep change" or "slow death." *Leading Through Learning, 13*(2). Available at www.pdkintl.org/publications/ Sparks_090309.pdf.

Table 4.1 STAGES OF CONCERN

STAGE OF CONCERN	DESCRIPTION	TYPICAL COMMENTS	SAMPLE INTERVENTIONS
STAGE 6 Refocusing	Refines one's collaborative learning practice.	• "Our effectiveness as a team would be enhanced if we occasionally had a full-day meeting for comprehensive data analysis and planning, the kind we can't get done in a 45-minute meeting."	• Meet with the principal and/or district staff to make your request. Be ready to identify the benefits and outcomes you want, make suggestions for how the refinement might work, and suggest what you hope the person will do to support your request.
STAGE 5 Collaboration	Seeks to engage with others to share experiences with collaborative professional learning.	• "I wonder if our team meetings are like other teams'. What are they doing that we can learn from? What can we share that works for us?"	• Suggest to the principal or leadership team that teachers have schoolwide opportunities to showcase each team's work. • Recommend that teams bring a sample agenda, planning sheets, logs, products, a videotape of their collaborative work, lessons learned, tips for success, etc. • Ask to visit another team in action. In a schoolwide faculty meeting, use the Success Analysis Protocol, **Tool 11.5** on the CD, to share work.
STAGE 4 Consequence	Examines the impact of collaborative professional learning on one's teaching practice and student learning.	• "How is this kind of collaboration impacting our teaching and student learning?" • "What evidence do we have that we are making progress?" • "One way the learning team is helping me is by sharing the responsibility for preparing so I don't feel so overburdened."	• Lead a conversation at lunch in which teachers share what they are gaining from collaborating with their peers. • Ask the school leadership team and/or principal to share data from reviewing team plans and the evidence of their results. • Ask team leaders to meet individually or collectively with the principal to periodically review their teams' work.

Table 4.1 STAGES OF CONCERN, continued

STAGE OF CONCERN	DESCRIPTION	TYPICAL COMMENTS	SAMPLE INTERVENTIONS
STAGE 3 Management	Wants to know how to manage time and resources associated with collaborative professional learning.	• "How will we ever have time for this?" • "What can we possibly do in that time that will make a difference?" • "I have so many other things to do. I am not sure when I'll get my lessons planned and papers marked."	• Describe how collaborative professional learning increases shared responsibility for instructional planning. • Describe how you manage time, and share how your collaborative professional learning team works. • Invite the individual to observe your collaborative professional learning team. • Offer to cover the person's class so he or she can observe a team.
STAGE 2 Personal	Wonders how collaborative professional learning will affect him or her.	• "What does this mean for me?" • "Does this mean more meetings?"	• Share your personal experience with learning teams. • Describe some of the personal, not professional, benefits. • Ask what specific concerns the speaker has and speak only to those. (Hint: Most are self-oriented concerns.)
STAGE 1 Information	Seeks more information about collaborative professional learning.	• "I'd like to know who is doing it." • "What is it exactly?"	• Identify people who might share information. • Offer resources for more information, answer questions, or share your experience with learning teams. • Share a video.
STAGE 0 Awareness	Has heard about collaborative professional learning, yet expresses no interest in knowing more.	• "I have heard about that."	• Acknowledge the response. • Offer to answer questions. • Recommend a resource for more information.

TOOL INDEX

TOOL	TITLE	USE
4.1	School's orientation to change	Tool 4.1 is a reflection task that asks individuals then small groups to characterize the school's orientation to change.
4.2	10 do and don't assumptions about change	Tool 4.2 describes strategies for school leaders to lead successful change.
4.3	Three articles beginning with 'I Love Lucy' teaches about change	Tool 4.3 includes an activity that uses a video to talk about change and how people respond to it, as well as two activities to help people understand the impact of change.
4.4	Competing values form obstacles to change	Tool 4.4 offers suggestions for understanding why people resist change.
4.5	8 forces for leaders of change	Tool 4.5 offers school leaders and leadership teams important guidelines on how to leverage change.
4.6	Shhhhh, the dragon is asleep and its name is Resistance	Tool 4.6 describes a three-step process for managing resistance that includes understanding why it occurs.
4.7	A measure of concern	Tool 4.7 offers information on CBAM and 10 ideas for handling resistance.
4.8	Anticipate change: Design a transition meeting	Tool 4.8 helps leaders understand how to establish a formal transition from what was to what will be.

Chapter 5

SCHEDULING
time
for collaborative
professional
learning

WHERE ARE WE NOW?

Our school includes time during the contract day for teachers to work together in teams whose members share common goals (school, grade level, department, etc.) for student learning.

STRONGLY AGREE   AGREE   NO OPINION   DISAGREE   STRONGLY DISAGREE

In our school, professional development occurs primarily during the school day.

STRONGLY AGREE   AGREE   NO OPINION   DISAGREE   STRONGLY DISAGREE

In our school, teams of teachers have scheduled time several times per week for professional learning.

STRONGLY AGREE   AGREE   NO OPINION   DISAGREE   STRONGLY DISAGREE

Our principal uses staff meetings for professional development.

STRONGLY AGREE   AGREE   NO OPINION   DISAGREE   STRONGLY DISAGREE

The leadership team (including the principal and teacher leaders) in this school ensures that time for collaborative professional learning is used to impact teaching and learning.

STRONGLY AGREE   AGREE   NO OPINION   DISAGREE   STRONGLY DISAGREE

The most effective professional learning experiences are job-embedded, collaborative, and connected to the real world of teaching and learning. Collaborative professional learning occurs during the workday, in the workplace, is connected to the real work of teaching and student learning, and includes all the teachers all the time.

Learning teams:

- Meet every day;

- Assume collective responsibility for all students the team serves;

- Use student content standards;

- Develop powerful lessons and common assessments;

- Critique student work;

- Observe and coach in one another's classrooms; and

- Determine needs for additional learning.

In schools where collaborative professional learning occurs, teachers have both formal and informal opportunities each day to learn how to help students achieve at higher levels. In these schools, small groups of teach-

NSDC standard

Resources: Professional learning that improves the learning of all students requires resources to support adult learning and collaboration.

ers meet to analyze data and decide which areas need to improve. Teachers routinely deliberate about new instructional strategies. Their workroom conversations focus on solving persistent classroom problems.

This kind of professional learning requires time within the workday. NSDC advocates that 25% of an educator's work time be invested in professional learning and that districts invest about 10% of their budgets. While those numbers may seem high, they are not — if professional learning occurs through daily collaboration.

Often in districts, professional learning occurs outside of educators' regular workday and involves guest speakers or external consultants coming into the school or district on days when students are not present, in the summer, or after school. In these cases, the costs for extra teacher compensation for time beyond their workday, consultant fees, and travel can be very high. Costs for these occasional, short-term opportunities for professional learning typically do not produce returns in terms of student achievement.

However, if professional learning involves teams collaborating during the workday and the costs include a portion of teachers' salaries for their time devoted to learning, the resources they might need, and a portion of the principal's salary for time spent supporting the team, then 10% of the budget is not unreasonable.

The same is true for the recommendation regarding hours. If professional development occurs only after school or in the summer, districts are unlikely to have educators who spend 25% of their work time on learning. However, including teachers' daily interactions with colleagues in collaborative professional learning teams during planning times and in designated team time makes it more likely that districts can achieve the recommended level. In fact, opportunities for learning occur virtually every minute. Experiences or incidents of the workday can be transformed into learning time when teachers engage in reflective collaborative practice, share their experiences with others, analyze the results of their actions, plan with their colleagues, and make their practice transparent to themselves and others.

The Resources standard in NSDC's Standards for Staff Development calls for time for:

- Daily individual lesson planning, review of student work, and preparation of materials;
- Team learning three to four days a week that includes analyzing student work, identifying student needs, developing lessons to increase student learning, and reflecting on classroom practice;
- Weekly school improvement committee meetings to analyze student achievement data, determine school improvement goals, plan for professional learning related to student learning needs, and re-

view progress on goals; and

- Whole-school learning once or twice a month in which faculty analyze student achievement data, prioritize goals, celebrate progress, recognize accomplishments, share successes, and build collaborative relationships.

Most educators cite time as their No. 1 barrier to implementing collaborative professional learning teams. Many schools have not yet adjusted their schedules to accommodate collaborative learning; however, more and more schools and districts across the country have reshaped their schedules to allow for job-embedded, collegial professional development during the contract day.

> **NSDC advocates that 25% of an educator's work time be invested in professional learning and that districts invest about 10% of their budgets.**

The schools that are making time usually do so in one of three ways: using available time, buying time, or adding time. Each of these options requires that schools be creative, be willing to make tradeoffs, be clear about the connection between teacher learning and student learning, and be willing to experiment with multiple approaches (Richardson, 2002). No single strategy works in all sites. Local and district policies prohibit some solutions, but allow others. **Tools 5.5** through **5.10** show how these schools and districts have crafted time for job-embedded professional development.

Teachers' willingness to work in collaborative professional learning teams varies. In districts and schools where teachers work in a supportive culture, they meet in collaborative teams for professional learning about teaching and student learning because they experience firsthand its benefits. In districts and schools where relationships are less collegial and a culture of isolation and competition exists, teachers may be less willing to work collaboratively during their planning time and might be particularly reluctant if no additional time is provided.

Building support to transition to collaborative professional development can be challenging. Teachers' past experience with professional development and the school's culture, trust, and relationships all influence teachers' willingness to work actively to make time for professional learning. Educators also should not underestimate the need to garner support from staff, parents, school board, and the community for changed time schedules. More than one school or district has been stymied by a backlash from parents and community members about new schedules, especially when those schedules involve early dismissals or late starts for students.

A task force that studies and makes recommendations to staff, parents, community, and school board is a powerful strategy that engages stakeholders in understanding the rationale and need for schedule changes. Nine steps help educators gain stakeholder support for new time schedules (Killion, 2006) that support collaborative professional development.

1. Form a task force.

Form a task force to study possibilities for finding time and generate recommendations for others to review. Because some options will affect students and parents, the task force may include parents and student representatives. School task force members will want to examine district and state policy regarding the length of the school day, district and state policy regarding time for professional development, and how the school or district currently uses professional development time.

When creating a charge for the task force, the principal needs to make clear the task force's level of authority, purpose, and timeline for completing the work. For example, will the task force make a single recommendation to the principal? Is the task force expected to bring

multiple recommendations for the staff to consider? Will the task force make the decision after sharing its recommendations, gathering input, and revising the recommendations based on the input from faculty and parents? Use **Tool 5.1**, the Task Force Charge Statement, included on the CD with the tools for this chapter, to clarify expectations, timelines, and responsibilities.

2. Explore current beliefs about time.

A beginning point for discussing time for collaborative professional development is considering how personal beliefs and culture influence one's thinking about time. One way to explore these issues is to read **Tool 5.2**, "Time use flows from school culture." Time use within a school is a very personal issue. Task force members or the whole staff can surface their assumptions about how time is used in their school.

3. Analyze current time use.

One of the easiest ways to structure time for collaborative professional development is to use existing time differently. Once the task force analyzes how time currently is used, members can recommend how to use time differently to allow collaborative professional learning. For example, one way to make time for job-embedded learning is to use faculty meetings. In some schools that designate one day a week for meetings, the principal can use one of the weeks each month for a faculty meeting, but allow teachers to meet in their collaborative teams on the other weeks. Another version of this model is to save faculty meeting time and bank the time into a longer block, either biweekly or monthly.

4. Establish and prioritize criteria.

Adjusting the schedule is a significant decision that can have a broad impact beyond the school. The task force may find it helpful to establish criteria for making the decision. For example, some school staff agree to adjust their schedule if it means maintaining the same amount of instructional time for students. Others agree to change the schedule if they retain a minimum amount of individual planning time, or they may want their professional development time only during the school day or teachers' contract day. Staff members consider, too, the community's needs and response to altering the school day schedule. Many communities respond negatively to altering the school schedule, so engaging community members in the decision and working with community agencies to identify alternatives for student supervision if students will be out of school are important considerations. Whatever the parameters, identify them early in the process. Sometimes not every criterion can be met, so prioritize the criteria, as well. A weighted matrix may aid in the decision making (see **Tool 5.4**).

5. Study other schools' and districts' solutions.

One way to determine how to make time for additional collaboration is to study what other schools and districts have done. **Tools 5.5 through 5.10** are included on the CD to help school task forces study possibilities for finding time. Not all the ideas suggested in these resources are feasible in every school or without some adaptation; however, all of the ideas are currently being used in a school. The resources offer ideas and possibilities to help schools get started.

6. Form recommendations.

After studying the possibilities, the task force forms recommendations for the school, including short-term changes, long-term changes, or both. For example, some schools begin by using existing time differently for a year before moving to a schedule change that permits more frequent time for professional learning. Once the task force develops recommendations, the principal,

central office staff, teacher union leaders, parent group leaders, community leaders, and other key leaders review the recommendations to ensure that they fall within regulations, contracts, etc.

7. Present recommendations for input.

Once the various groups have reviewed the recommendations, the task force presents them to the larger school community for review and feedback. The task force, school leadership team, or school administrators will want to work closely with parents to develop their understanding of the benefits of extending time for teacher collaboration. Developing a knowledgeable parent community also will help lessen any criticism of the proposed changes. Task force members should be sure that any recommendations presented to the staff and community meet most of the established criteria and either comply with regulatory criteria or are permissible through variances.

Task force members take an active role in explaining possible changes and their rationale to stakeholders, requesting feedback from staff and community members about each recommendation. Task force members, who have contributed extensive time researching the topic, may find this step difficult, so it is helpful for them to ask stakeholders to structure their feedback to include positive aspects, areas of concern, and alternatives. The task force then can compile and review the feedback as part of the refinement process.

8. Revise the recommendations.

The task force considers all the feedback and refines the recommendations. Members may delete, combine, significantly revise, or moderately revise some recommendations to reflect the feedback. The task force may want to archive all the recommendations in order to revisit other options.

Task force members then prepare a presentation of

REFLECTIONS

1. Who will be the biggest supporters of a new time schedule? How can they be prepared to continue to give support and build support among other stakeholders?

2. Who will be the biggest critics of a new time schedule? How can their concerns be included in the school/district's deliberations about time for professional development?

3. Because of past experience with traditional workshop activities, some educators will not see the value in changing the schedule to allow more time for professional development. What could you do to ensure that faculty members understand that the new schedule allows educators to enhance their opportunities for collaboration during the workday?

4. What kinds of effort do you believe are needed to gain support from key stakeholders for a new schedule?

5. What obstacles exist in the school/district culture that would hinder efforts to change the schedule?

the final recommendation(s) for the entire school community. Depending on how the group was chartered, it may make a single recommendation to another body for approval, make the decision, or present multiple recommendations for approval by one or more persons.

9. Determine action.

The task force uses the appropriate process within the school or district for making decisions such as this, and the decision-making body accepts or rejects the final recommendation(s). Depending on the outcome, the task force then creates an action plan to implement the decision.

Creating a new schedule is only the beginning of the story. Once time is available for job-embedded professional development, educators need help to use this time well. Documenting how the time is used and the effects on teaching and learning is important, both for ongoing evaluation and for ongoing support. In some school districts where new schedules were created, school boards have rescinded the decision when the

time was not used to improve teaching and learning and the district could not demonstrate its value for teacher or student learning.

While creating a new schedule that supports collaborative professional development is a monumental task, the next step is to form a task force to study and identify collaborative activities and protocols. This task force may meet during the newly scheduled time. Experiences across the country show that unless staff have the capacity to use this time well, it can be lost. Chapter 11 can help educators learn about structured collaborative tasks.

REFERENCES

Killion, J. (2006). *Collaborative professional learning in school and beyond: A tool kit for New Jersey educators.* Oxford, OH: New Jersey Department of Education and NSDC.

Richardson, J. (2002, August/September). Think outside the clock: Create time for professional learning. *Tools for Schools,* 1-2.

TOOL INDEX

TOOL	TITLE	USE
5.1	Task force charge statement	Tool 5.1 provides a format and sample task force charge statement. This tool clarifies the expectations and responsibilities of task force members.
5.2	Time use flows from school culture	Tool 5.2 includes the article, discussion questions, and a discussion protocol to structure a productive faculty discussion around a highly charged topic.
5.3	Analysis of current time usage with time use log	Tool 5.3 provides a matrix that helps faculty examine how time is currently used for professional development.
5.4	Criteria sort with weighted matrix	Tool 5.4 provides a description and sample of a weighted criteria matrix that task force members can use to help in their decision making.
5.5	Think outside the clock	Tool 5.5 is an issue of *Tools for Schools*, a newsletter of the National Staff Development Council. It includes articles on how schools and districts around the country have made time for professional development.
5.6	Time enough for teaching and learning	Tool 5.6 is a newsletter of the Alabama Best Practices Center that provides articles about how schools across Alabama have created time for professional learning.
5.7	Making time for adult learning	Tool 5.7, an article from the *Journal of Staff Development*, describes how schools and districts built time into the daily schedule for teacher learning.
5.8	Finding time for teams	Tool 5.8 is an article that describes how one school district was able to work with key stakeholders to provide 30 hours of professional development within the school year and within the school day without changing the teacher contract.
5.9	Shaping the workday	Tool 5.9 describes multiple strategies that provided teachers more time to work together on their own learning.
5.10	4 places to dig deep to find more time for teacher collaboration	Tool 5.10 describes how schools can find time within the existing schedule for teachers to work together.
5.11	Comparisons of strategies for making time for collaborative professional learning	Tool 5.11 is a matrix that helps task force members summarize how various schools and districts have created new schedules for professional learning, how much time they created, and processes for exploring whether each strategy meets the task force's criteria.
5.12	Forming a recommendation	Tool 5.12 helps a task force include the most essential information in its recommendations for making time for job-embedded professional development.

Chapter 6

THE ROLE
of central
office

WHERE ARE WE NOW?

Central office staff provide resources for school-based, collaborative professional learning.

STRONGLY AGREE   AGREE   NO OPINION   DISAGREE   STRONGLY DISAGREE

The district comprehensive professional development plan designates schools' use of collaborative professional learning.

STRONGLY AGREE   AGREE   NO OPINION   DISAGREE   STRONGLY DISAGREE

Central office staff share knowledge, research, and best practices about professional learning broadly and widely throughout the district with principals and teachers.

STRONGLY AGREE   AGREE   NO OPINION   DISAGREE   STRONGLY DISAGREE

Central office staff tailor district-provided professional development to support the goals included in schools' professional development plans.

STRONGLY AGREE   AGREE   NO OPINION   DISAGREE   STRONGLY DISAGREE

Central office staff understand how they support schools in the area of professional learning.

STRONGLY AGREE   AGREE   NO OPINION   DISAGREE   STRONGLY DISAGREE

A decade ago, professional development experts began to describe a necessary shift that school systems would be required to make to guarantee powerful, effective professional development for their teachers, the kind of professional development that leads to improved student learning. With this shift, central office staff have a new role — to build the capacity of school-level personnel to design, manage, and implement improvement efforts.

When it comes to educational reform, the individual school now is the "center of change" (Fullan & Stiegelbauer, 1991, p. 203). In other words, the school — not the district — needs to be in control of planning and implementing change. In his meta-analyses of educational research, Robert Marzano (2003, p.10) found that "the school (as opposed to the district) is the proper focus for reform. Indeed, this is a consistent conclusion in the research literature."

Yet Marzano's finding should not be misinterpreted to mean that district-level staff have no responsibility for school-level change. The district administrator's charge is to "develop the management capabilities of

> "Today, the concept of job-embedded staff development has come to mean that educators in many roles — superintendents, assistant superintendents, curriculum supervisors, principals, and teacher leaders — must all see themselves as teachers of adults and must view the development of others as one of their most important responsibilities. These individuals are increasingly being held accountable for their performance as planners and implementers of various forms of staff development."
>
> — *Sparks & Hirsh, 1997, p. 83*

administrators — other district administrators and principals — to lead change" according to Michael Fullan (2007, p. 229). Neither top-down nor bottom-up strategies are adequate to leverage desired changes in schools and classrooms. Centralized (top-down) change seems not to work because it uses a uniform or one-size-fits-all approach "that is inappropriate and ineffective except for the narrowest of goals" (Fullan &

Stiegelbauer, 1991, p. 200). Decentralized (bottom-up) change can be difficult, he says, because of the "lack of capacity to manage change" (p. 200). Fullan and Stiegelbauer suggest that a combined effort between schools and central office will most likely result in increased learning for students. The most effective change strategy includes "co-management, with coordination and joint planning enhanced through the development of consensus between staff members at all levels about desired goals for education" (Louis, 1998, p. 161). Only districts with this kind of collaborative change strategy will successfully implement school improvement projects. Fullan and Stiegelbauer also remind district administrators that their goal is not to install a specific program but to "build the capacity of the district and the schools to handle any and all innovations" (1991, p. 214).

"Effective central offices do not simply monitor whether schools comply with an endless set of rules," says Richard Rothman, editor of VUE (2009). "Instead, they work with schools to provide needed resources and support and reach out to community members and organizations to find additional sources of support. They are nimble and flexible, rather than hidebound. And they make decisions by using data and research."

Every school system seems to have "isolated islands of excellence," according to Wendy Togneri and Stephen Anderson (2003), individual schools populated by incredible instructional leaders and inspiring teachers who cause all their students to learn at high levels. The challenge for district leadership is to ensure that each school is equally ready to accept and accomplish the same goal. As Togneri and Anderson report (2003, p. 23-24), districts that adopted job-embedded professional development:

- **Used research-based principles to define professional development.** Principles that guided their work included using data to identify the content of

professional development and employing a variety of professional development designs to provide ongoing support for teachers to implement new classroom strategies.

- **Developed networks of instructional experts.** Central office focused on developing teachers' and principals' instructional leadership skills. District staff understood that each school needs in-house expertise in order to improve instructional practices. Principals were essential to this work, as were teacher leaders. The most viable approach was a combined effort of the principal and teachers.

- **Developed a support system for new teachers.** Central office found that retaining new teachers was a priority goal. Districts developed mentoring programs and other support systems to assist new teachers.

- **Strategically allocated financial resources.** The superintendent, school board, central office, and principals prioritized goals in order to focus their efforts on activities that would make the biggest difference in improving student performance. Districts spent funds strategically on instructional improvement and student achievement goals.

- **Encouraged and assisted schools in using data.** Central office staff provided schools with high-quality data and with technical assistance on how to use that data to guide instructional practices.

The National Staff Development Council has created a set of Innovation Configuration (IC) maps to describe the role of central office staff in implementing high-quality professional learning. The IC maps identify the major outcomes for each of NSDC's Standards

> NSDC has created a set of Innovation Configuration maps to describe the role of central office staff in implementing high-quality professional learning.

for Staff Development. They also describe a continuum of practices that begins with ideal or high-quality implementation and ends with nonuse. Two underlying assumptions of IC maps are that change is incremental and that high-quality implementation of new practices will have greater impact than using new practices at a lower level of quality. IC maps can be used as a self-assessment instrument to compare current behaviors to ideal practice. These IC maps, included on the CD that accompanies this book, explain the central office staff role in promoting collaborative professional learning.

CENTRAL OFFICE RESPONSIBILITIES

When professional development moves from a centralized function in a school district to a school-based function, central administrators' work actually increases. The nature of the work changes — from determining content and delivering the learning to building school staffs' capacity to make sound decisions about their own professional development. In essence, central office staff become learning leaders who are responsible for facilitating professional development decisions at individual schools and coordinating efforts between and among schools to maximize resources and effort without diluting individual schools' needs and interests.

> The school staffs' success depends largely on how well the central office has prepared them to make sound decisions.

In addition, central office administrators are responsible for coordinating the formation of cross-school teams for singleton teachers or noninstructional staff whose primary collaborative professional learning team is outside their own school. Central office staff members — those who work in school district offices with responsibility for curriculum, instruction, professional development, mentoring, teacher quality, and student success — have seven major tasks in a system that views the school as the primary center of learning. They:

- Build the capacity of school staff to make sound decisions about professional development;
- Provide research and models of best practices regarding professional development;
- Allocate resources to schools to support school learning plans;
- Coordinate efforts between and among schools;
- Coordinate the formation of cross-school collaborative professional learning teams;
- Support collaborative professional learning teams; and
- Monitor implementation throughout the district.

Build capacity

When professional development moves from the district office to the school and becomes more collaborative, the control central office has exerted over decisions about how to design and implement professional development now rests in the hands of teachers and principals. The school staffs' success, however, depends largely on how well the central office has prepared them to make sound decisions.

Central office staff are responsible for helping school staff members understand the standards for professional development and district and state requirements for professional development. If those making the decisions about professional development have limited understanding and experience with high-quality staff development, their decisions will reflect the forms of professional learning with which they are most familiar. As a result, professional learning may have limited impact on teaching and student learning.

Transferring knowledge can happen in a variety of ways. One is to train a team of teacher leaders and administrators at each school in the standards and in professional development planning, design, and evaluation.

Because school-based, collaborative professional

development requires knowledge and skills that school staff members may not have, central office can provide opportunities for teacher leaders, especially department chairs, team, or grade-level chairs, to participate in leadership training that would prepare them to lead collaborative learning teams within their schools. These learning experiences would help teacher leaders gain the capacity to facilitate learning teams, lead effective meetings, manage multiple priorities, and plan quality learning for their colleagues. Central office staff can work with principals to identify candidates among teachers who can serve as leaders among their peers.

Central office also can facilitate professional development planning, design, implementation, and evaluation processes at school sites with a school-based co-facilitator. This facilitator works alongside the central office staff member to learn about critical decision areas and how to lead decisions about professional development at the school.

Central office staff can take an active role in helping school staff implement the Backmapping Model (Killion, 2002a, 2002b) provided in Chapter 9 to ensure that learning teams' work focuses directly on student learning. The Backmapping Model is a process to ensure that professional development aligns with the school's goals for student achievement. Although some teachers may be outside their school for professional development because their collaborative team exists elsewhere, these teachers' primary emphasis still is on improving learning in their own school. Central office staff might use the Backmapping Model to help school staff members understand how to develop both school- and team-based professional learning and to expand teacher leaders' and principals' understanding of high-quality professional learning.

Transferring knowledge and skill from a few central people to a broader group makes it more likely teachers and principals will be confident and successful

in examining adult learning needs within their school. The more broadly the knowledge is shared, the greater the likelihood that more educators will take responsibility for ensuring high-quality professional learning and for linking professional learning to student learning.

Provide research and model best practices

When professional learning moves to the school, central office staff can significantly impact the quality of school-based decisions about professional learning by providing schools with research and sharing best practices.

Central office staff members play a significant role in supporting school-based learning by compiling and disseminating research and resources about professional learning to teacher leaders and principals. By summarizing or sending articles, policy papers, studies, or examples about best practices to school leaders and team facilitators, central office staff can increase the likelihood that school faculty will have foundational information to use to make local decisions about professional learning.

> **Central office also can facilitate professional development planning, design, implementation, and evaluation processes at school sites with a school-based co-facilitator.**

District staff also can engage school professional development committee members in learning about multiple designs for professional learning. Chapter 11 describes a variety of designs for collaborative professional learning.

These powerful forms of professional learning will allow school staff to see examples of different approaches to learning, and they will become more familiar with alternatives to consultant-driven training.

Allocate resources

District staff can help schools succeed with collaborative professional learning by advocating for time for teams to work together (see Chapter 5) and fiscal resources to support this form of adult learning.

Districts can help schools revamp daily schedules to include time for professional learning. Districts also help develop support for job-embedded time. Districts and schools need to prepare teachers to talk within the community about the importance of continuously developing their knowledge so that teachers can help build community support for and understanding of the value of professional development. The educators most closely in touch with the community can help parents understand the link between quality professional development and every parent's desire for his or her children to have the most qualified teachers possible. The central office is responsible for working through the school board to build community value and support for professional learning.

> **Central office staff can benefit schools by identifying and broadcasting successful practices within the district.**

In addition, a significant portion of the district's responsibility is supporting the school's staff development committee as it plans for collaborative professional learning. Districts can form teams charged with examining policies, administrative procedures, practices, resources, and schedules that impact professional development to ensure that the district matches actions to words in supporting school-based professional learning. Finally, districts can ensure that schools receive appropriate budget allocations to support high-quality professional learning.

Coordinate efforts between and among schools

An essential central office function for supporting collaborative learning in schools is coordinating efforts between and among schools. Central office staff review each school's professional development plan to determine the plan's strengths, whether it meets professional development standards, whether it aligns with the school's and district's improvement goals, and whether the school has allocated appropriate resources.

Central office also is responsible for assisting schools in developing an efficiency of scale. Because school-based collaborative professional learning focuses on an individual school's needs, one school often does not know when others in the district are working on similar areas of improvement. When central office staff bring common goals to the attention of all schools working on that goal, the potential for schools collaborating on improvements rises, benefiting each individual school by encouraging the schools to share their learning, resources they have discovered, or solutions that are working. Central office staff also might streamline support by serving schools clustered together by professional learning goals rather than trying to provide support one-by-one. Schools can use opportunities for cross-school collaboration to review each other's plans as a way to improve professional learning in each school.

Central office staff can benefit schools by identifying and broadcasting successful practices within the district. Individual schools will appreciate knowing about professional learning in other schools so they can learn from others and have opportunities to benchmark their professional learning plans against other schools within the district and beyond.

Coordinate cross-discipline or cross-school teams

Staff such as counselors, librarians, nurses, and others sometimes will not have colleagues at their school focused on the same content and so will not have a natural team in their own school. These staff have opportunities to create cross-school teams, district teams, interdisciplinary teams, or related content-area teams within a school based on identified student needs. For example, world language teachers, particularly when there is only one per language, might meet in cross-school teams facilitated by the district curriculum specialist to focus on developing curriculum and assessments appropriate for that language. Noninstructional staff, such as nurses, counselors, social workers, etc., might also meet in cross-school teams to address topics unique to their interactions with students and staff. In these examples, teachers who may be the sole subject instructor within a school have opportunities to be a part of a role-specific, collaborative learning team. In another example, librarians from schools throughout a district may form a collaborative professional learning team to identify how to support classroom reading instruction within their library programs.

Central office can foster collaboration for those educators who are not members of an in-school collaborative professional learning team by organizing interschool visitations within the district or across districts. Central office staff members work with principals to identify staff members who may benefit from cross-school, cross-discipline, or cross-district teams. By initiating and coordinating cross-school, districtwide, or even regional teams, central office staff members ensure that every professional is involved in one or more collaborative professional learning teams that focus on student success, core curriculum content standards, assessment, and instruction.

Support collaborative professional learning teams

By charting the schools and looking at a synthesis of their professional learning intentions, central office staff members can quickly see where the clusters are and plan accordingly to provide necessary support.

Central office can then determine a course of ac-

tion by asking schools these questions:

- How can central office help a school and its learning teams or cluster of schools with the same goal achieve that goal? What essential support services, resources, assistance, etc., do the schools and their teams need to be successful? What differentiated support might the cluster of schools or teams from within schools need?
- What systemwide changes in policy, resources, procedures, or structures are needed for schools to successfully achieve their goals?
- How do we help schools learn about and access district resources to meet their goals?
- How do school goals align with district priorities?

Monitor implementation

Central office holds schools accountable for their professional learning plans. Central office staff meet with school leadership teams quarterly or semiannually to review evidence of schools' progress toward their professional learning goals, helping schools focus on results and not just providing services. By reviewing progress and asking schools to use data to focus on results, the district will be able to help schools celebrate their successes and alter their courses of action when necessary.

When data are used, decisions are likely to be more objective than subjective.

When data are used, decisions are likely to be more objective than subjective. One means of gathering data is through monitoring visits. These can be a walk-through, a form of brief observation designed to gather data and to encourage reflection. One or more central office staff members or teams that include principals and teacher leaders from other schools can conduct monitoring visits. Monitoring visits include debriefing sessions with the school's professional development team, leadership team, and/or whole faculty to offer

REFLECTIONS

1. What assumptions do central office staff members make about schools as the center of learning for students and adults? What do they see as the advantages and disadvantages of more school-based professional learning?

2. In what ways does a central office support collaborative professional learning in its schools? What are some examples of how central offices demonstrate support?

3. What policies and procedures about professional learning might need to change in the district to support more school-based, collaborative professional learning?

4. How does central office engage school leaders in implementing collaborative professional learning?

5. What additional support can central office staff provide schools?

support, feedback, and the perspective of critical friends to help the school stay the course.

Using data from multiple sources is important so that facts — and not opinions and preferences — guide the district's discussion and are the basis for identifying successes.

Identify and provide organizational support

"Effective professional development, however, depends heavily on the presence of school and district leaders who encourage teacher learning through teacher community and collaboration, support shared leadership and teacher autonomy in instructional content and pedagogical methods, and allocate resources in ways responsive to and supportive of teachers' efforts to enhance the learning, understanding, and achievement of their students."

— *Adam Gamoran, 2005, p. 8*

District leaders may have more responsibility for providing the organizational support to help school leaders implement collaborative professional learning. Schools making the transition to a new approach to professional learning benefit from increased district

support. Some forms of organizational support that districts provide are to:

- Prepare principals and teacher leaders to facilitate learning teams;

- Provide school leaders the flexibility to make critical decisions related to their daily schedules, budget, calendar, staffing, and governance to ensure shared leadership;

- Make relevant data easily accessible to school leaders and provide the appropriate development in using data effectively;

- Create a districtwide resource bank via a district portal or other means using current research on professional learning that is linked to student achievement;

- Conduct ongoing school-based support in the form of walk-throughs, coaching for school leadership teams and the school principal, and ongoing feedback and evaluation.

District leaders make a difference in whether schools successfully implement collaborative professional learning. While some schools are able to make the transformation to collaborative professional learning

Figure 6.1

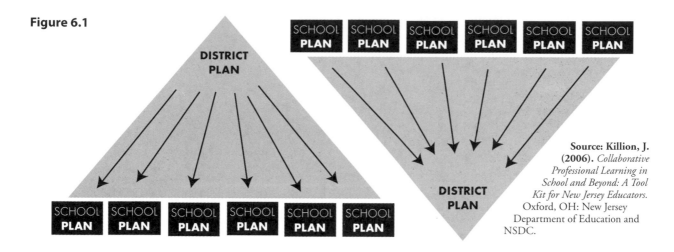

Source: Killion, J. (2006). *Collaborative Professional Learning in School and Beyond: A Tool Kit for New Jersey Educators.* Oxford, OH: New Jersey Department of Education and NSDC.

without district support, the presence of intensive support from the district signals the district's commitment to increasing teacher capacity and student learning. District staff need to identify and provide these supports to encourage and sustain any priority change effort. **Tool 6.8** on the CD helps district and school leaders identify specific organizational supports for local programs.

SUPPORTING COLLABORATIVE LEARNING

Rather than being a top-down or one-size-fits-all approach to professional learning, school-based professional learning looks at the unique needs of each school and its students, staff, and community and responds to those differences.

The role of central office staff members does not diminish when a school district transforms professional learning from a centralized function to one that is school-based and that fosters collaboration among teachers about the real work of teaching. In fact, their role expands as they become learning leaders who facilitate school-based decisions about professional learning to meet the unique and pressing needs of individual schools.

In this model, the work of the district professional development committee expands from organizing a few

inservice days for the entire district to ensuring a comprehensive system of professional learning for every teacher aligned with the identified needs of each school.

The district's professional development plan, then, reflects how the district will support individual schools' professional development plans. The new method of professional development planning looks like an inverted triangle (see **Figure 6.1**) in which the districtwide plan emerges from individual schools' plans rather than the district dictating schools' professional learning choices.

This change from district-driven professional learning to school-based professional learning is not one that will occur overnight. Districts are transforming their services and responsibilities to support school-based professional learning while working to maintain alignment with and focus on district priorities and goals. District office staff have a tremendous responsibility to prepare school teams to design, implement, and evaluate sound professional learning aligned to district and school goals.

REFERENCES

Fullan, M. (2007). *The new meaning of educational change* (4th ed.). New York: Teachers College Press.

Fullan, M. & Stiegelbauer, S. (1991). *The new meaning of educational change.* New York: Teachers College Press.

Gamoran, A. (2005). Organizational capacity for change: Rethinking professional development. *Professional Development from the Inside Out: District and School-Level Strategies,* a newsletter of the Comprehensive Center-Region VI, *8*(1), 8-10.

Guskey, T. (2000). *Evaluating professional learning.* Thousand Oaks, CA: Corwin Press.

Killion, J. (2002a). *What works in the elementary school: Results-based staff development.* Oxford, OH: NSDC & NEA.

Killion, J. (2002b). *What works in the high school: Results-based staff development.* Oxford, OH: NSDC & NEA.

Louis, K. (1998). The role of the school district in school improvement. In M. Holmes, K. Leithwood, D. Musella (Eds.), *Educational policy for effective schools* (pp. 145-67). Toronto, Ontario, Canada: OISE Press.

Marzano, R. (2003). *What works in schools.* Alexandria, VA: ASCD.

Rothman, R. (2009, Winter). The new "central office." *Voices in Urban Education, 22.* Available at www.annenberginstitute.org/VUE/winter09/Rothman.php.

Sparks, D. & Hirsh, S. (1997). *A new vision for staff development.* Alexandria, VA: ASCD.

Togneri, W. & Anderson, S. (2003). *Beyond islands of excellence: What districts can do to improve instruction and achievement in all schools.* Alexandria, VA: ASCD.

TOOL INDEX

TOOL	TITLE	USE
6.1	New role for central office	Tool 6.1 challenges central office staff members to consider their role in supporting school staff in implementing collaborative professional learning.
6.2	Innovation Configuration maps: Central office staff members	Tool 6.2 describes the roles and responsibilities of central office staff in the implementation of NSDC's Standards for Staff Development. It focuses on how central office staff can support school-based work.
6.3	Boost the learning power of school-based staff	Tool 6.3 describes the use of Innovation Configuration maps for central office staff and the role central office plays in building a system that supports collaborative professional learning at the school.
6.4	'Letting go' is essential for growth	Tool 6.4 provides a rationale for the use of collaborative learning. It can be used to begin district-level conversation about the need for job-embedded, collaborative professional learning.
6.5	Districts can make a difference	Tool 6.5 describes why central office needs to build the capacity of school-based staff in order to implement more effective professional learning.
6.6	School professional development plan synthesis	Tool 6.6 provides a useful tool for district staff to summarize schools' professional development goals to find commonalities among building plans.
6.7	Articles from *The Learning System*	Tool 6.7 describes how the central office can build capacity among teachers and principals about effective professional learning.
6.8	Identifying organizational support	Tool 6.8 can be used by administrators and teachers to identify organizational supports needed within their system related to job-embedded professional learning.
6.9	When hearts meet minds: District's leadership team uses the power of synergy in work with principals	Tool 6.9 describes how a local district built collaborative learning structures and individual support to boost principal learning.

Chapter 7

THE ROLE
of the principal

WHERE ARE WE NOW?

Our principal demonstrates his/her support for collaborative professional learning.

STRONGLY AGREE   AGREE   NO OPINION   DISAGREE   STRONGLY DISAGREE

Our principal develops teacher leaders' skills and knowledge in planning and designing school-based professional development.

STRONGLY AGREE   AGREE   NO OPINION   DISAGREE   STRONGLY DISAGREE

In our school, when teachers meet in small teams, the principal trusts them to accomplish their goals.

STRONGLY AGREE   AGREE   NO OPINION   DISAGREE   STRONGLY DISAGREE

Our principal provides regular feedback to teams about their learning plan and progress.

STRONGLY AGREE   AGREE   NO OPINION   DISAGREE   STRONGLY DISAGREE

Our principal provides the resources and support teachers request to build and sustain collaborative professional learning.

STRONGLY AGREE   AGREE   NO OPINION   DISAGREE   STRONGLY DISAGREE

To say that the success of collaborative professional learning rests in the principal's hands may be overgeneralizing, but to a large degree, it is true. Principals' commitment, investment, and involvement are essential for collaborative professional learning to succeed within a school. To create, organize, and sustain collaborative professional learning, principals have several essential responsibilities. Principals:

- Nurture teacher leaders;
- Identify and provide organizational support;
- Set clear expectations and define results;
- Create time for collaboration in the schedule;
- Provide training and development;
- Receive and review team plans;
- Give feedback on team actions and results;
- Encourage "out-of-the-box" thinking;
- Handle resistance; and
- Accept that change is a process, not an event.

Nurture teacher leaders

Along with high-quality teaching, the principal's role is one of the most crucial elements affecting student achievement. Effective leaders create trust within the system, share responsibility for student learning, and develop a school culture that fosters collaborative professional learning opportunities.

While the principal's instructional leadership helps create and maintain a schoolwide focus on student learning, principals are increasingly aware that they need support to meet growing administrative and leadership responsibilities. Through collaborative professional learning, principals share leadership for professional learning and offer viable opportunities to teachers ready to accept leadership responsibilities.

Standards for school leaders, established by the Council of Chief State School Officers and the National Association of Elementary School Principals, describe distributed leadership as a core value and skill for members (CCSSO, 1996; NAESP, 2003).

The principal needs to value and deploy the knowledge that exists within the building. Teachers have developed expertise in many areas, and principals need to activate these skills to solve schoolwide problems and issues. The principal needs to harness the staff's skills and talents to solve problems, identify barriers, and plan actions to attain school goals. Establishing a professional culture where each educator is expected to learn from and with colleagues may be the first step in developing and employing staff skills.

Implementing school-based, collaborative professional learning requires principals to reflect on their leadership behaviors and determine whether they are developing allies within the school who hold the same vision for collaborative professional learning. As Dennis Sparks, NSDC's emeritus executive director, notes (2002, p. 7-2):

"Principals are expected today to create learning communities in their schools and to engage the broader school community in creating and achieving a compelling vision for its schools, which typically serve increasingly diverse student populations. They are asked to give up 'command-and-control' views of leadership and to be instructional leaders steeped in curriculum, instruction, and assessment who can coach, teach, develop, and distribute leadership to those in their charge."

No success in a school, no matter what it is, lies exclusively on the principal's shoulders. Teachers and teacher leaders are integral to every achievement and share responsibility for leadership. Effective principals work to share leadership throughout the system so that there are many leaders working hand-in-hand to meet the school's goals.

Identify and provide organizational support

"Many improvement efforts in education fail simply because they are unclear or misleading about the kind of organizational support required for change. As a result, educators end up trying to implement innovations that they do not fully understand in organizations that do not fully support their efforts."

— *Guskey, 2000, p. 149*

A lack of organizational support for change is like

carbon monoxide — it is a silent killer of innovation and improvement. This axiom seems true for any organization. Thomas Guskey (2000) summarized organizational conditions and resources critical to successfully implementing new processes, practices, and policies:

- Subject-specific materials such as leveled reading books, mathematics manipulatives, science experiment equipment;
- Access to colleagues who are also using the innovation;
- Classroom evaluations that support the use of the innovation;
- An administrator or supervisor who is knowledgeable and supportive of the innovation;
- Time to support the use of the innovation;
- Protection from outside intrusions that might divert energy, time, and attention from implementation;
- Openness to experimentation — a trusting environment;
- Recognition of success and of progress;
- Support at all levels of administration; and
- Support by colleagues.

> "We found clear evidence that the administrator is key to the existence of a professional learning community."
> — *Grace Fleming (in Hord, 2003, p. 20)*

When these conditions exist, change is more likely to happen. When they do not exist, efforts to change and improve wither. The principal and teachers, working together, need to identify what organizational supports are needed within their context to create effective collaborative professional learning, and the principal is responsible for providing the supports that encourage and sustain change efforts.

Set clear expectations and define results

Principals are responsible for establishing clear expectations about teacher collaborative professional development. Working in partnership with teacher leaders, principals clarify who will be involved in collaborative professional development: every staff member, some staff, or just those who volunteer. Principals also clarify whether teachers are expected to collaborate in one or more than one team within the school, across schools, in the district, or across districts.

> **"Principals were not expected to lead alone, and teachers were not expected to work in isolation."**
>
> — *Togneri & Anderson, 2003, p. 23*

Some schools expect that teachers will meet with one collaborative learning team related to their content area or level and another that is focused on a schoolwide area of interest. For example, a middle school music teacher might meet with other music teachers across the district for her content-focused team. This learning team works to analyze curriculum, develop common assessments, examine student work, and develop common units of instruction. The same music teacher also meets with a school team to work on infusing critical thinking into all classes. In the latter team, the music teacher works with colleagues from other disciplines in her school to identify the critical thinking skills they will stress at each grade level, develop their own understanding about how to integrate these skills into their classroom activities, and develop recommendations for other peers about how to integrate these skills into their classes.

Principals also define expected results. Working with each team and using a data analysis process as background, the principal helps each team understand how its actions can influence student success. By stressing that the primary purpose of collaborative professional learning is student academic success, principals help teachers focus their collaborative work. When teachers successfully build a collaborative culture, they experience the benefits of deepened content knowledge and expanded content-specific pedagogical repertoire. Principals can monitor the learning process for all of these results.

Create time for collaborative professional learning in the schedule

One of the most significant contributions a principal can make to successful collaborative professional learning is providing time within the workday for teachers to collaborate. Chapter 5 addresses this issue in greater depth. The principal has primary responsibility to form a task force to study options for making time available and serves as the spokesperson within the community to advocate for time in the workday for teacher learning. The principal cannot turn over this responsibility to an assistant or a group of teacher leaders. He or she must be fully present and involved in these actions to signal the issue's importance.

Provide training and development

Teachers don't magically begin to collaborate. Collaborative professional development teams benefit from initial opportunities to learn about the value of collaborating, essential skills for developing teams, and strategies for teaming. By providing opportunities for teacher leaders or even the entire staff to learn some of the foundational knowledge and skills necessary to successfully collaborate, principals increase the likelihood of a smooth transition to this new form of professional development.

Receive and review team plans

Principals review each team's plans for learning, provide feedback to the team, discuss with members how to provide the resources and support they request, and help them accomplish their plan. Principals visit team meetings periodically to learn about the team's work and to offer support. The team and principal need to develop ongoing communication to keep the principal informed, provide information about what the team is learning to share with other teams in the school, and to focus each team on results that achieve the school's goals.

Give feedback on team actions and results

Douglas Reeves (2006) describes leadership actions that link to student achievement. These actions do not depend on a principal's style or personality, but on what a principal does, according to Reeves. They include:

- **Inquiring:** using data to determine not only problems but also underlying causes (see Chapter 10);
- **Implementing:** the degree to which aspects of a specific effort are correctly implemented at the school and classroom level; and
- **Monitoring:** the way in which feedback is provided to continuously support improvement and equity. This form of monitoring, Reeves notes, is not evaluating or measuring, but rather paying attention to what matters to ensure it stays in the forefront of everyone's daily work.

Principals actively monitor team actions and results. They do this primarily by reviewing team meeting logs. However, principals may meet with team leaders or with teams to learn about their work and provide feedback on the work, results (such as data from student common assessments or benchmark exams), and members' interactions. Through regular feedback, principals and teams clarify expectations, improve their work as a team, and are more likely to focus on work that will improve teaching and learning.

Encourage "out-of-the-box" thinking

Principals encourage teams to look beyond members' own knowledge, skills, and practice. Principals connect team members with print, human, or electronic resources that will move them past their current

understanding and introduce them to new ideas, approaches, and strategies. When principals take an active role to ensure teams have access to resources, they stimulate teachers' learning and demonstrate their confidence in team members' ability to achieve their goals. Principals also have an important role in creating a safe environment that encourages teachers to take risks, experiment, and learn from each trial. Effective principals understand that experiences that do not produce the intended results might be more powerful for learning than those that do.

Handle resistance

Most teachers, once they have worked through the challenges of shifting from outside in to inside out professional learning, value collaborative learning, especially if the focus of their learning is directly related to their own classes and students. However, some resistance is inevitable. Some teachers will be uncomfortable collaborating. A few will believe initially that collaborative professional learning means additional work. Others simply prefer to work in isolation because they always have. Principals, when establishing expectations, clearly communicate each teacher's responsibilities so that no confusion exists. They prepare for teachers unwilling to participate in collaborative learning teams and anticipate how they will handle such resistance. Chapter 4 describes strategies for handling resistance.

> Working with each team and using a data analysis process as background, the principal helps each team understand how its actions can influence student success.

Accept change as a process, not an event

When collaborative professional learning is launched in most schools, there is a period of adjustment for everyone. As teams learn to work together, to

REFLECTIONS

1. What skills, knowledge, and capacities do school staff members need in order to be able to implement collaborative professional development?

2. This chapter describes high expectations for principals. How ready are principals for these changes?

3. What opportunities are available for principals to learn how to lead and facilitate collaborative professional learning within their schools?

4. This chapter describes an expanded role for teacher leaders. Are principals interested in and prepared for such a change? What steps might principals take to build teachers' capacity for leadership?

5. How do school leaders create a culture of trust and risk-taking within the school?

be more responsible for their own professional learning, to make good choices about how to use their time, etc., principals have an important role to provide training, support, and coaching to teams. Principals remind teams that nothing is perfect immediately, that teams will feel uncomfortable and even be unsuccessful initially, and that they will improve their effectiveness and efficiency over time. This means principals' standards for teamwork change as teams mature and their work becomes more focused. The principal is ready to step in to facilitate, guide, teach, and/or provide resources, support, or resource personnel to help all teams reach an acceptable level of productivity.

CONCLUSION

Principals may use the series of essays by Dennis Sparks, NSDC's emeritus executive director, (**Tool 7.1** on the CD) to help them consider the benefit and their role in creating a culture for collaborative professional learning within their schools. Other tools for this chapter include the benefits of collaborative professional learning, key learnings for collaborative professional learning teams, and strategies for principals to increase

staff capacities for continuous learning.

Each of the 12 NSDC's Standards for Staff Development has leadership behaviors connected with it. A set of Innovation Configuration (IC) maps includes a thorough description of those behaviors (**Tool 7.12** on the CD). According to Gene Hall and Shirley Hord (2001), IC maps identify the major components of an innovation and describe a continuum of practices that begins with ideal or high-quality implementation and ends with nonuse. Two underlying assumptions of IC maps are that change is incremental and that high-quality implementation of new practices will have greater impact than using new practices at a lower level of quality. Principals can use the IC maps as a self-assessment instrument to compare their current behaviors with ideal practice.

REFERENCES

Council of Chief State School Officers. (1996). *Interstate School Leaders Licensure Consortium: Standards for school leaders.* Washington, DC: Author.

Guskey, T. (2000). *Evaluating professional development.* Thousand Oaks, CA: Corwin Press.

TOOL INDEX

TOOL	TITLE	USE
7.1	Essays by Dennis Sparks	Tool 7.1 describes the principal's role in developing a climate that supports collaborative professional learning. The essays also describe the benefits of collaborative learning for adults and students.
7.2	Benefits of collaborative professional learning	Tool 7.2 lists the benefits of collaborative professional learning drawn from Shirley Hord's research about professional learning communities.
7.3	Collaborative professional learning team walk-through guide	Tool 7.3 is a walk-through tool principals can use in short visits to collaborative learning teams to gather data and provide feedback to staff members and teams.
7.4	A learning community is built on trust	Tool 7.4 is a brief article about the role of trust in learning communities.
7.5	Leadership actions that help teams flourish	Tool 7.5 includes two activities to help school leaders examine their role in developing successful learning communities.
7.6	Key learnings for collaborative professional learning teams	Tool 7.6 is a list of essential skills and knowledge for principals to consider in designing training and development for teams and/or team leaders.
7.7	Principals' strategies for increasing staff capacities for continuous learning	Tool 7.7 describes techniques that focus faculty on continuous learning. (continued)

Hall, G. & Hord, S. (2001). *Implementing change: Patterns, principles, and potholes.* Boston: Allyn & Bacon.

Hord, S. (2003). *Learning together, leading together: Changing schools through professional learning communities.* New York: Teachers College Press.

National Association of Elementary School Principals. (2003). *Leading learning communities: What principals should know and be able to do.* Washington, DC: Author.

Reeves, D. (2006). *The learning leader: How to focus school improvement for better results.* Alexandria, VA: ASCD.

Sparks, D. (2002). *Designing powerful professional development for teachers and principals.* Oxford, OH: NSDC.

Togneri, W. & Anderson, S. (2003). *Beyond islands of excellence: What districts can do to improve instruction and achievement in all schools.* Alexandria, VA; ASCD.

TOOL INDEX, continued

TOOL	TITLE	USE
7.8	In the right context	Tool 7.8 describes how principals establish structures that support collaborative professional learning.
7.9	Culture shift doesn't occur overnight — or without conflict	Tool 7.9 describes ways the principal shifts the school culture and some roadblocks he or she may face in the process.
7.10	How to launch a community	Tool 7.10 shares lessons a principal learned as she formed a professional learning community within her school.
7.11	Getting everyone to buy in	Tool 7.11 describes how one principal launched collaborative learning within his school.
7.12	Innovation Configuration maps: The principal	Tool 7.12 includes a selection of Principal IC maps related to NSDC's professional development standards, plus a description of how these maps could be used to self-assess current practices.
7.13	Assessing your role as instructional leader	Tool 7.13 is a quick self-assessment for principals to determine the extent to which their behaviors match those of strong instructional leaders.
7.14	Three strands form strong school leadership	Tool 7.14 addresses three strands necessary for strong school leadership.

Chapter 8

THE ROLE
of the coach

WHERE ARE WE NOW?

Our school has a coach who supports teachers in refining their teaching.

STRONGLY AGREE	AGREE	NO OPINION	DISAGREE	STRONGLY DISAGREE

District coaches are available to support our school's implementation of collaborative professional learning.

STRONGLY AGREE	AGREE	NO OPINION	DISAGREE	STRONGLY DISAGREE

Teacher leaders facilitate team meetings.

STRONGLY AGREE	AGREE	NO OPINION	DISAGREE	STRONGLY DISAGREE

Our school coach attends team meetings to support members' learning.

STRONGLY AGREE	AGREE	NO OPINION	DISAGREE	STRONGLY DISAGREE

Our school leader coaches teams of teachers.

STRONGLY AGREE	AGREE	NO OPINION	DISAGREE	STRONGLY DISAGREE

When implementing a new way of learning and working together, schools benefit from the support of skillful coaches. Whether these coaches are full-time, part-time, or even occasional visitors, coaches serve an important role in shaping how successful schools implement collaborative professional learning.

They work with both teachers and school leaders to develop an understanding of collaborative professional learning, assist teams to implement processes to learn and work together, and provide teams with ongoing coaching to refine their collaborative learning and work.

Coaches are teachers who serve in a leadership role primarily facilitating school reform and improving teaching quality. They may have a formal leadership role, such as department chair, academic associate, grade-level leader, or instructional coach or facilitator. Both their titles and scope of work vary, yet their primary purpose is to help teachers individually and in teams as they engage in their work. Coaches' work supporting collaborative professional learning takes on multiple forms.

> When the school does not have a coach, the principal can fill the role.

COACHING ROLES

Taking the Lead: New Roles for Teachers and School-Based Coaches (Killion & Harrison, 2006) outlines 10 roles for coaches. Each of these roles, outlined in **Table 8.1**, helps those who lead from within to support their colleagues in meeting their professional goals.

When schools are making the transition to collaborative professional learning or refining their existing practice, coaches have a special role working with teams of teachers rather than individuals. In this way, they exponentially increase the impact of their work. While coaching teams, they focus on the processes and structures teams establish; interactions among team members; climate and culture of teams; team effectiveness in using the cycle of continuous improvement to shape their learning and collective work; their goals and ability to assess those goals; and their results. When the school does not have a coach, the principal can fill the role. The principal can act as a coach, developing teams' capacity to be effective both as a group and in individual learning and results.

While all coaching roles are essential, some are particularly helpful as a school is transforming its professional learning to a collaborative, team-based approach. The roles of data coach, learning facilitator, and catalyst for change can support teachers and school leaders in implementing and refining collaborative professional learning.

Data coach

As data coaches, school- or district-based coaches help teams gather and use data. Coaches use the Learning School Innovation Configuration Map (**Tool 14.5** on the CD) to talk with teams about their work and their effectiveness. They use various team effectiveness assessments to help the team sharpen its processes for learning and interacting to improve results. Coaches help teams identify indicators of success and benchmarks for their goals, and they facilitate conversations about the data collected to measure progress toward the team's SMART (specific, measurable, attainable, results-oriented, and time-bound) goals. Coaches can use the tools in Chapter 10 to facilitate data conversations with team members and tools in Chapter 14 to facilitate team effectiveness assessments.

Coaches are in a unique position to assess the overall effectiveness of collaborative professional learning because they periodically meet with all or most teams. They can use data gathered from observing many teams in action and from the types of support teams request to identify patterns of success and challenges. Together with team facilitators, the school leadership team, and school leaders, coaches can identify the types of support needed and address barriers, problems, and concerns in a timely manner. They can use the expertise of teams that have succeeded to help teams that are not quite ef-

fective by highlighting practices that work. Coaches can encourage team leaders to pair up to learn from one another when one has a challenge the other has already addressed. Coaches can lead team facilitators in action research and study groups to address challenges that are more widespread.

Learning facilitator

As learning facilitators, coaches help school staff members understand what collaborative professional learning is and how it works. Together with the leadership team and school administrators, they use tools such as those in this book to assess where to begin their work. They help teams carefully examine the definition of collaborative professional learning and compare it to the teams' current work. **Table 8.2** suggests strategies for teams and schools at different stages of collaborative professional learning.

Catalyst for change

As catalysts for change, coaches courageously speak the truth and identify areas for change. They state their points of view, make observations based on data, and request changes. Their moral compass points true north — toward success for students through quality teaching. They challenge teams of teachers to set SMART goals and identify pathways to achieve those goals. They help teams identify indicators of success and benchmarks for their goals, along with ways to collect evidence to assess their progress. Coaches meet with team facilitators to challenge them to expand what team members know and are able to do as teachers. They encourage team facilitators to address issues within their teams that may be in-

> Coaches are in a unique position to assess the overall effectiveness of collaborative professional learning because they periodically meet with all or most teams.

terfering with success.

In the landmark research that resulted in the Concerns-Based Adoption Model (CBAM), Gene Hall and Shirley Hord (2001) describe how different school leaders have unique functions in facilitating and promoting change. Their research revealed several different ways facilitators of change influenced or promoted change. The first change facilitator, often the formal leader —

> **School-based coaches become a part of the leadership team with responsibilities to support and lead change.**

the principal — within a school, influences change through a particular set of behaviors that differed from those of other change facilitators. The second change facilitator, assistant principals, coaches, or teacher leaders, promotes change from somewhat different approaches. The third change facilitator, teacher leaders if they were not second change facilitators, has slightly different functions. External change facilitators, often someone from the district office, can support change, although to a lesser degree than leaders within the school. **Table 8.3** summarizes each change facilitator's behavior that research has demonstrated has a greater a level of importance in influencing change.

Among the functions Hall and Hord (2001) cite as important for second change facilitators, such as coaches, are:

- **Reinforcing:** Speaking positively about the change; encouraging those who are participating in collaborative professional learning teams; reminding colleagues about the importance and benefits of collaborative professional learning teams.

- **Providing technical coaching:** Providing opportunities to develop team members' knowledge and skills for effective collaborative professional learning so that implementation of collaborative professional development is smooth; training, modeling,

offering practice opportunities; providing ongoing assessment of the knowledge and skills team members need.

- **Monitoring:** Regularly assessing how collaborative professional learning is working; determining what is working and what needs to be adjusted; addressing problems; celebrating successes.

- **Following up:** Keeping promises; orchestrating opportunities for cross-team sharing and learning; encouraging individual and team collective responsibility to the team's and school's goals.

School-based coaches become a part of the leadership team with responsibilities to support and lead change. Yet they often also are teachers with a strong allegiance to those colleagues striving to provide the highest quality teaching every day for every student. Having influence with principals and teachers gives coaches tremendous opportunities to find leverage points to effect significant change. Coaches, because they interact closely with the principal, can communicate what teachers need for effective teaching. They also can communicate school goals and vision to teachers in their interactions with them, keeping the focus on teaching quality and student achievement.

ASSESSING THE COACH'S EFFECTIVENESS

In change initiatives, clarifying school leaders' roles and responsibilities accelerates change, helps with distributing leadership, and builds capacity more quickly. However, coaches sometimes have no reference point to help them determine whether what they are doing is advancing quality teaching and student learning. Because districts typically do not outline role expectations for coaches or guide their daily work, coaches must look for indicators to help them assess their effectiveness.

Innovation Configuration (IC) maps for coaches and school-based teacher leaders related to several of NSDC's Standards for Staff Development can help

REFLECTIONS

1. What role or roles defined in **Table 8.1** does our school coach play? What roles are needed?

2. How does our school's coach support teams in improving their practice and results?

3. Looking at **Table 8.2**, what stage has our team reached? What needs to occur for us to reach the next level?

4. In the absence of a coach, who besides the principal supports the teachers as they refine their instructional practice?

5. Who acts as a facilitator of change in our school? Whose responsibility is it to facilitate change? Which behaviors are most evident in their leadership of the change? How do the various change facilitators collaborate to lead change in our school?

those engaged in practicing an innovation know how to improve by describing the behaviors in levels that approach the ideal. In this way, a person involved with the innovation can see where he or she falls in relationship to the ideal and can use the progression along the IC map to strategize about how to move close to that ideal.

Four of the 12 maps that appear in *Taking the Lead: New Roles for Teachers and School-based Coaches* (Killion & Harrison, 2006) are included in **Tool 8.2.** The four maps are for learning community, design, collaboration, and quality teaching. Coaches can use these tools to assess their practices in supporting collaborative professional learning teams. Coaches also can use the maps to set professional goals to refine their support of learning teams.

REFERENCES

Killion, J. & Harrison, C. (2006). *Taking the lead: New roles for teachers and school-based coaches.* Oxford, OH: NSDC.

Hall, G. & Hord, S. (2001). *Implementing change: Patterns, principles, and potholes.* Boston: Allyn & Bacon.

Table 8.1 ROLES OF COACHES

Roles	Description	Examples of support for collaborative professional learning teams
Resource provider	Collects and shares print and nonprint resources to support instruction, planning, assessment, or team effectiveness.	• Selects two assessments of team effectiveness from *Becoming a Learning School* to use with the team to help improve members' collaborative work. • Brings web-based resources to the team to help members integrate 21st-century skills into their unit plan. • Shares a protocol with the team for responding to text. • Offers an article to the team that provides ideas for managing classrooms.
Data coach	Facilitates access to and use of data to plan instruction and assess progress toward team goals.	• Teaches team members how to analyze data and to conduct root cause analysis. • Facilitates a data conference for the whole school to examine the school's results on state assessments. • Guides teams in using data to write SMART goals for student learning.
Curriculum specialist	Focuses support on using the adopted curriculum to plan instructional lessons or units and assessments of and for learning.	• Engages team members in understanding the key knowledge and skills embedded within a standard. • Helps team members understand how to use the curriculum documents to differentiate instruction for students who are above or below expected levels. • Shares curriculum resources, including pacing guides and indicators of learning to plan daily lessons and learning goals. • Helps teachers map curriculum for the school year or course so that the expected curriculum is addressed.
Instructional specialist	Facilitates decisions about which teaching strategies to use to meet learning outcomes; helps team members understand the impact of different instructional practices; helps teachers plan for differentiation and accommodations to meet the learning needs of all students.	• Engages teachers in a discussion about which high-yield instructional strategies will best accomplish unit goals. • Offers assistance to plan ways to adjust instruction of students with special learning needs, including English language learners, students with disabilities, etc. • Helps teachers identify effective strategies to engage students in the learning process. • Offers ideas for monitoring learning during instruction so teachers can make adjustments as needed.
Classroom supporter	Provides classroom-based support, including modeling teaching, co-teaching, or observing with feedback to assist teachers as they refine instructional practices.	• Conducts demonstration lessons for individual or teams of teachers and debriefs after the lesson to discuss the instruction and student learning. • Plans and co-teaches; debriefs to reflect on the effectiveness of the teaching. • Conducts grand rounds by leading a team of teachers to observe in classrooms for short or extended periods, and engages teachers in reflection about observed practice.

Table 8.1 ROLES OF COACHES, continued

Roles	Description	Examples of support for collaborative professional learning teams
Mentor	Guides novice teachers in teaching, meeting professional expectations, working collaboratively with their peers, working with families and community, and working with school and district leaders.	• Facilitates collaborative teams of novice teachers focused specifically on instructional and classroom management topics to accelerate their learning. • Guides novice teachers in the protocols and procedures more experienced teachers use in collaborative professional learning teams. • Assists novice teachers in addressing concerns they have about collaborative professional learning, especially concerns related to inequity in teams.
Learning facilitator	Facilitates informal and formal learning experiences to extend teachers' content knowledge and instructional practices and their effectiveness in collaborative professional learning teams.	• Leads training for the whole staff on the cycle of improvement to strengthen teams' effectiveness. • Uses resources in *Becoming a Learning School* to develop a schoolwide understanding of collaborative professional learning. • Brings team facilitators together to share new text-response protocols to use in team meetings. • Develops teams' understanding of various designs for professional learning.
School leader	Contributes to school reform efforts by serving as a formal team leader, a member on various committees or task forces, or supporter of reform efforts.	• Facilitates the school improvement team. • Serves as co-facilitator with the department chair of the algebra teachers' team. • Serves as a member of the school resource staff collaborative professional learning team. • Leads others by exhibiting a positive attitude about collaborative professional learning. • Listens to those who express resistance to collaboration to understand their perspectives.
Catalyst for change	Seeks to engage colleagues in change by speaking honestly about student learning; brings "undiscussables" to the appropriate forum; identifies barriers.	• Engages colleagues in dialogue about their beliefs and assumptions. • States his or her point of view, and asks others for theirs. • Makes observations about practices that are contradictory with the goals. • Keeps the vision alive by speaking about goals and plan of action. • Finds common ground or small steps toward the vision, and engages others in acting on them. • Celebrates successes.
Learner	Models learning and continuous improvement by engaging in formal and informal learning.	• Attends workshops or conferences to strengthen coaching practices. • Participates in a collaborative professional learning team with other coaches or teacher leaders. • Reads professional material to build capacity for learning and coaching. • Shares what he or she is learning with others.

Table 8.2 COACHING STRATEGIES FOR DIFFERENT STAGES OF COLLABORATIVE PROFESSIONAL LEARNING

Stage	Characteristics	Strategies for coach-as-learning-facilitator
Beginner	Has not yet started collaborative professional learning or is in an early stage.	• Provide training on what collaborative professional learning is. • Share research on collaborative professional learning. • Lead a book study on the Collaboration and Teacher Expertise chapters from *The Learning Educator*. • Show NSDC's video on the definition of professional learning (available at www.nsdc.org/standfor/definition.cfm). • Engage teams of teachers in a discussion about what collaborative professional learning is and is not (use **Tool 1.5**).
Novice	Time has been set aside for teams to meet, yet teams are uncertain how to best use their time.	• Teach the cycle of continuous improvement using the NSDC video, *Professional Development in Action*, an example of collaborative professional learning (available at www.nsdc.org/standfor/definition.cfm). • Offer a workshop for the faculty on the cycle of continuous improvement and ask teams to report out where in the cycle their work currently is. • Invite teams that have had more success to share their strategies at a faculty meeting.
Proficient	Teams are working together, establishing plans, and using some protocols for learning.	• Offer teams additional learning designs to add variety and depth to their learning process. • Invite teams to assess their effectiveness using one of the tools in Chapter 14. • Meet with the team to talk about its successes and challenges. • Have a team meeting in a fishbowl at a faculty meeting, and facilitate a discussion about the team's learning and effectiveness. • Meet with team facilitators to solve problems of practice.
Advanced	Teams are producing results for students, are using the cycle of continuous improvement, are challenging the status quo, and are demonstrating success for all students.	• Videotape the team in action and debrief the meeting with team members, inviting them to look for ways to strengthen their work. • Meet with team facilitators and share with them advanced protocols. • Facilitate inter-team visitations so teams can learn from one another. • Facilitate cross-team showcases and share lessons learned.

Table 8.3 FUNCTIONS OF CHANGE FACILITATORS

First change facilitator		Second change facilitator		Third change facilitator		External change facilitator	
Formal leader; principal		Formal leader such as assistant principal and/or coach		Teacher leaders such as grade-level, team, or department chairs or facilitators of collaborative professional learning teams		District professional development coordinator; curriculum specialist; school improvement specialist	
Sanctions	• • • •	Reinforces	• • •	Provides technical coaching	•	Serves as liaison	• • •
Keeps priorities straight	• • • •	Provides technical coaching	• • •	Reinforces	•	Provides resources	•
Provides continued help	• • •	Monitors	• • •	Models	•	Offers expert knowledge about the innovation	•
Provides resources	• • •	Follows up	• • •			Functions as a workshop trainer for innovation nonusers, users, and site change facilitators	•
Monitors	• •	Sanctions	• • •			Coaches and mentors first and second change	•
Reinforces	• •	Provides resources	• •			Facilitates	•
Pushes	• •	Trains	• •			Conducts implementation assessment and evaluation studies	•
Tells others	• •	Pushes	• •				
Approves adaptations	• •	Tells others	•				
Provides technical coaching	• •	Approves adaptations	•				

• = degree of importance of each role.

Source: Hall, G. & Hord, S. (2001). *Implementing change: Patterns, principles, and potholes.* Boston: Allyn & Bacon.

TOOL INDEX

TOOL	TITLE	USE
8.1	Coaching request form	Tool 8.1 is a form for teams to use to request coach support (available in both Word and PDF).
8.2	Innovation Configuration maps	Tool 8.2 includes four of the 12 Innovation Configuration maps for school-based coaches and teacher leaders that can be used for personal reflection, assessment, and setting professional goals.
8.3	Team professional learning plan	Tool 8.3 is a planning guide for coaches to use as they assist teams in developing and implementing professional learning to achieve their goals.
8.4	Lesson planning	Tool 8.4 guides coaches in facilitating lesson planning sessions with teams.

PART 3

Strategies for success

Chapter 9

PLANNING
effective professional learning

WHERE ARE WE NOW?

We identify the focus of our professional development by analyzing a variety of student achievement data.

STRONGLY AGREE   AGREE   NO OPINION   DISAGREE   STRONGLY DISAGREE

The focus of our professional development aligns with our school improvement goals.

STRONGLY AGREE   AGREE   NO OPINION   DISAGREE   STRONGLY DISAGREE

Our professional development goals are written in a SMART goal format and stipulate what improvements we want in teachers' knowledge, skills, and practices.

STRONGLY AGREE   AGREE   NO OPINION   DISAGREE   STRONGLY DISAGREE

We selected new instructional strategies based on evidence of improved student learning.

STRONGLY AGREE   AGREE   NO OPINION   DISAGREE   STRONGLY DISAGREE

Our professional development plan includes long-term support strategies that help teachers implement new classroom practices.

STRONGLY AGREE   AGREE   NO OPINION   DISAGREE   STRONGLY DISAGREE

To paraphrase American psychologist Abraham Maslow, if all you have is a hammer, everything starts to look like a nail. In the field of education, workshops remain the hammer in the professional development tool kit. Despite 25 years of research that has identified the limitations of this training model, most schools answer every adult learning need by finding a presenter and planning a workshop.

School improvement plans and professional development should complement and be aligned with each other.

Creating and sustaining effective classroom practices that improve student learning require a different set of tools. However, merely replacing workshops with another form of professional development, such as learning teams or action research, is not enough. Change the hammer and change the nail — take time to determine student learning needs and what educators need to know and be able to do before planning professional development.

Analyzing and diagnosing student and adult learning needs will lead to very different forms of professional learning. For example, if teachers analyze student learning data and find students are not performing well in reading comprehension of expository text, they next need to determine whether expository reading material is available in classrooms and what teaching strategies best help students comprehend this kind of text. A workshop might be appropriate if teachers do not know how to help students develop strategies to comprehend expository text. If teachers have already been exposed to appropriate instructional strategies but are not implementing them, then professional learning could take place in grade-level learning teams that support teachers in developing common lesson plans, reviewing student work, and observing each other's classroom instruction.

The Backmapping Model for Planning Results-Based Professional Learning in **Figure 9.1** describes a seven-step process for planning professional learning (Killion, 1999). Districts, schools, departments, or grade-level teams can use this process, but adult learning is likely to more closely align with student needs when school or department or grade-level staff are re-

Figure 9.1 BACKMAPPING MODEL FOR PLANNING RESULTS-BASED PROFESSIONAL LEARNING

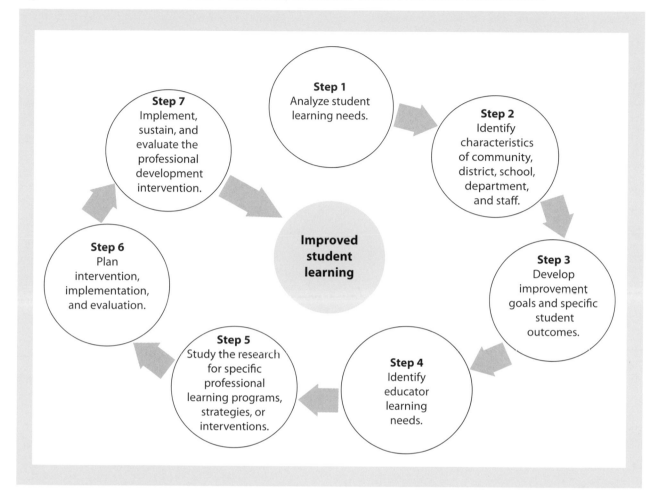

sponsible for analyzing the data and planning professional learning.

Some of these steps may seem familiar. They are, in fact, similar to most school improvement planning models. School improvement plans and professional learning should complement and be aligned with each other. School improvement plans identify student learning goals, while professional learning helps educators acquire the knowledge and skills to help students meet those goals. Depending on the district or school's current improvement process, this planning model may provide a few steps to add to established processes.

The backmapping model guides educators in planning results-based professional learning that improves student learning and achievement. In Step 1, educators identify student learning needs. Step 2 involves analyzing the department, school, and district context. In Step 3, planners develop an improvement goal that specifies improved student achievement as the end result and educator learning as a step in accomplishing the goals. Step 4 has educators identify adult learning needs and replaces the traditional needs assessment survey process. Step 5 involves reviewing research about possible strategies to ensure any program planned has evidence of its impact on student learning. In Step 6, the planning group selects the intervention and plans for its implementation and evaluation. Step 7 involves implementing, sustaining, and evaluating the professional development intervention.

Step 1: ANALYZE STUDENT LEARNING NEEDS.

To produce results, professional learning must be directly tied to student learning needs. Before selecting or designing professional development, carefully and thoroughly analyze student achievement data to identify specific areas of student achievement and areas of need. This analysis will help guide decisions about the format of professional learning.

Key questions to answer during this step include:
- What assessment data are available?
- What is being measured in each assessment?
- What areas of student performance are meeting or exceeding expectations?
- What areas of student performance are below expectations?
- What patterns exist within the data? How are the data similar or different in various grade levels, content areas, and individual classes?
- How did various groups of students perform? (Consider gender, race, special needs, English language learners, socioeconomic status.)
- What do other data reveal about student performance?
- What surprises us?
- What confirms what we already know?

The data analysis process results in staff knowing or identifying:
1. Specific areas of student need;
2. Specific knowledge and skills that students need in order to improve achievement; and
3. Specific students or groups of students for whom the need is most prevalent or pronounced.

For example, a school's scores on a state assessment are below the expected or desired level in mathematics.

These scores by themselves are insufficient to use for planning professional learning. Suppose the mathematics department faculty next analyze subtest and student group scores. They find a particular group of students is performing poorly in the area of probability and statistics. They then may review the curriculum to determine which standards or learning objectives are most essential for students to achieve and what fundamental knowledge and skills students may be lacking that serve as the prerequisites to these standards. Faculty then use this information to establish schoolwide and/or department improvement goals, identify specific actions necessary to achieve those goals, and guide the selection and/or design of a professional development intervention to address the need to increase the probability and statistics skills of the identified group of students.

In this example, simply identifying mathematics as a focus doesn't provide enough information for staff to design professional learning to address the problem. The more detailed skills and identified student groups provide actionable information that is specific enough for planners to identify what teachers need to know and be able to do in order to improve student performance in probability and statistics.

While state assessment data is important, any analysis should include other data. Consider district or school interim assessments, grades, attendance, discipline issues, graduation rates, demographics, and other student data. School and district staff also need strategies for analyzing student achievement data, identifying student learning needs, and translating student data into improvement goals.

Step 2: IDENTIFY CHARACTERISTICS OF COMMUNITY, DISTRICT, SCHOOL, DEPARTMENT, AND STAFF.

School leaders and teachers use what they know about students' characteristics to decide what instruction and programs are appropriate for them. The same is true for professional development leaders. Knowing the characteristics of the adults who will participate in professional learning influences the design of the learning experience and the nature of the follow-up support. For example, professional learning for experienced teachers may be different than professional learning for novices. A program for teachers working to meet the needs of urban, disadvantaged students may be different than one for teachers in rural schools. A program in a district or school with limited resources and/or time for professional learning will be different than in settings where time and resources are available. Detailing the context helps professional development leaders make informed decisions about appropriate professional learning.

Develop a profile of the school environment and conditions by considering these questions:

What are the characteristics of the students?
- Ethnicity/race
- Gender
- Socioeconomic status
- Mobility
- Family support
- Motivation
- Attitude toward school
- Experience in school
- Academic performance
- Retention rates
- Parents' education level
- Sibling data

What are the characteristics of the staff?
- Years of experience
- Years at grade level
- Years in the school
- Past experience with professional development
- Motivation
- Performance/ability
- Attitude
- Sense of efficacy
- Response to change
- Collegiality
- Extent to which teachers' preparation aligns with teaching assignments
- Level of education

What are some characteristics of formal and informal leadership for both teachers and administrators?
- Leadership style
- Roles of formal and informal leaders
- Level of participation in leadership activities
- Opportunities to be involved in leadership roles/activities
- Trust in leadership
- Support by leadership
- Support for leadership
- Level of communication

What are some characteristics of the community?
- Support for education
- Support for the school
- Involvement in school activities
- Support for students
- Support for professional development

What resources are available to support professional development?
- Budget
- Time
- Support personnel in the building
- Support personnel outside the building
- Union contract
- Incentives

Once the analysis is complete, use this information to consider which interventions are most appropriate for the school or team.

Step 3: DEVELOP IMPROVEMENT GOALS AND SPECIFIC STUDENT OUTCOMES.

Educators need to be clear about what students and teachers are to accomplish as a result of teachers' professional learning. Missing the mark is easy without a goal and specific target.

Key questions about outcomes include:

• What results do we seek for students?

• What new practices do we expect from staff?

The intended results of the professional learning should be stated in terms of student achievement. Teachers' and principals' actions or changes are the means to achieve the goal of increasing student achievement. For example, "100% of the staff will participate in training in brain-based learning" is not a goal because it does not describe the training's impact on student learning. Professional development goals too often state the activities that will be conducted rather than results to be accomplished.

> Educators need to be clear about what students and teachers are to accomplish as a result of teachers' professional learning.

A preferable goal or objective would be: "In three years, 90% of students will read on grade level as result of teachers learning and implementing new brain-based instructional strategies." This statement focuses on the end result of professional learning rather than on what occurs in the process. These objectives might state that a majority of teachers will use new practices routinely and with high quality or high fidelity. Student learning will only be affected when teachers implement new strategies well — not just know them.

Write clear and specific goals and objectives using the components of a SMART (specific, measurable, attainable, results-oriented, time-bound) goal format. (See **Tool 9.3** on the CD.)

Step 4: IDENTIFY EDUCATOR (TEACHER AND ADMINISTRATOR) LEARNING NEEDS.

Professional learning frequently begins with a needs assessment survey that asks adult learners to identify what they want to learn. This common practice often leaves a gap between what educators want to learn and what they may need to learn to address the identified student learning goals. **Tool 9.5** on the CD provides a rationale for eliminating the traditional needs assessment survey in favor of analyzing student learning needs. For example, teachers are often eager to learn about educational innovations, and principals may want to learn how to shortcut nagging managerial tasks. However, if the goal is to increase student reading performance, and students' greatest deficits are comprehending and interpreting informational text, teachers and principals need to develop their skills and knowledge about how to help students read nonfiction text. Professional learning on other topics takes time and resources away from the established school improvement and team learning goals.

Classroom walk-throughs are useful in determining what teachers need to learn. Walk-throughs help administrators and teams of teachers gather information about instructional strengths and needs and provide a framework for using that information to discuss instruction, monitor how professional development is implemented, and measure professional development's effect on classroom practices.

Classroom walk-throughs can give administrators clear information about teachers' current practices and help leaders identify trends and patterns of practice within a school or district. Administration and faculty can use the information to discuss effective classroom practices and determine what learning is needed to accomplish their student learning and professional learning goals.

After identifying educators' learning needs, consider what actions to take to meet these needs. The scope and content of the professional learning required will be clearer when student learning needs, the school or district's context and characteristics, the specific goal, and educator learning needs all are clear.

Step 5: STUDY THE RESEARCH FOR SPECIFIC PROFESSIONAL LEARNING PROGRAMS, STRATEGIES, OR INTERVENTIONS.

After establishing educator learning goals, examine the research for specific professional development practices that are supported by evidence of their impact on student learning. In their urgency and enthusiasm to improve student performance, school staff may pass over this critical step and select or adapt unfamiliar programs. They often fail to critically review available programs and practices to determine whether the new practices have proven successful. Sometimes, teachers within a school have conducted action research studies that can provide findings to consider when selecting interventions. Their findings can be reviewed at this step along with other research-based options.

Even well-designed, formal professional development initiatives need to be reviewed for their effect on student learning. NSDC has published a series of *What Works* books (Killion, 1999; Killion, 2002a; Killion, 2002b) that reviewed professional development programs in various content areas for elementary, middle, and high school levels. These books provide each program's evidence of impact on student learning.

For other programs, the professional development program review form (**Tool 9.7** on the CD) identifies essential questions important in collecting research-based evidence of results.

Once research-based options have been identified, consider these questions to narrow the choices:

- Which professional learning addresses the skills and knowledge we have identified as educator learning needs?
- What professional development are schools with similar student demographics using?
- If our school's characteristics do not match the schools in which the professional learning was successful, what are the key differences? How likely are those differences to interfere with the program's success? What changes might increase the likelihood of success?
- What aspects of the professional learning (if any) might need to be modified to accommodate the unique features of our school or students?
- What are the strengths and weaknesses of the professional learning?
- What school, district, and community support was required to make the professional learning successful?

Next, consider the school's context by asking:

- What are the characteristics of the culture and climate?
- What do teachers already know and what do they need to know next?
- What practices are teachers currently using in the classroom? How different are current practices from desired practices?
- Does the school culture embrace new practices or resist changes?
- What are teachers' current levels of understanding of content related to state standards?
- What support do teachers need in order to implement new strategies?

After examining research-based evidence and weighing the options, the context factors identified in Step 2 become criteria for selecting an intervention appropriate for the school, the staff, and the student population. Members decide to adopt or adapt an existing professional development program or to create one to align with their unique school characteristics, their goals, and current research.

This is a significant decision that needs to be made with careful thought and thorough discussion. When making this decision, members are determining where they will place their energy and resources for the long run.

Step 6: PLAN INTERVENTION, IMPLEMENTATION, AND EVALUATION.

Initiating new professional learning takes time and energy. To implement new professional development strategies requires that leaders or faculty plan follow-up or long-term support beyond the immediate school year. A professional development intervention needs to be carefully selected to match teacher learning needs. Many questions need to be answered to get the best fit between educator needs and appropriate professional development design. Many of the job-embedded professional development strategies can be used in combination to help educators learn about new practices, begin implementing new practices, and consistently use new practices. Each of these three aspects of learning new classroom strategies requires different kinds of professional learning. The ultimate goal is to enhance the instructional practices used in the classroom so that student learning is improved.

Powerful Designs for Professional Learning (Easton, 2008) includes 21 job-embedded professional development practices. Each strategy has information to help administrators and teachers decide when and why to use these strategies. This information helps school faculty determine which strategies might work best, fit a particular context, and lead to teachers learning specific content.

For example, some professional development strategies are most useful for:

- Gathering and using information from within the school or district about learning: Accessing Student Voices, Action Research, Classroom Walk-Throughs, Data Analysis, Portfolios for Educators, Shadowing Students, and Visual Dialogue.
- Creating professional learning communities: Critical Friends Groups, Mentoring, Peer Coaching, Tuning Protocols, and Visual Dialogue.
- Focusing on standards, curriculum, and assessment: Action Research, Assessment as Professional Learning, Case Discussions, Curriculum Design, Immersing Teachers in Practice, Lesson Study, Standards in Practice, Study Groups, and Visual Dialogue.
- Focusing on instructional practices or pedagogy: Action Research, Case Discussions, Critical Friends Groups, Immersing Teachers in Practice, Journaling, Lesson Study, Mentoring, Peer Coaching, Portfolios, and Tuning Protocols.

More detailed information about how to select appropriate professional learning designs to match the learning needs of teachers and administrators can be found in Chapter 11. Chapter 11 describes a variety of job-embedded professional learning strategies to use to develop awareness of new instructional strategies or programs, build knowledge, translate new knowledge into practice, practice using new strategies, and reflect on new practice.

After selecting, adapting, or designing a professional development program/intervention and before implementation, consider:

- What kind of support does the program need to be successful?
- How will we support the individuals involved?
- What are we equipped to do to support and implement the professional learning, and what external

REFLECTIONS

1. Consider the components of the backmapping model. Which of these steps are you currently using? How can you refine these activities to bring them into line with the model?

2. Where can you find research to support the adoption of new professional learning?

3. Who plans or designs professional learning for the district or school? How well-prepared are they to plan professional learning as described in this chapter? If they do not feel ready, who can help increase their capacity?

4. How many sources of student data do you have available for analysis? How comfortable are staff in conducting their own analysis of student data? What could be done to help them become more comfortable?

5. Step 6 of the backmapping process requires thoughtful planning and is typically the school's or district's first step. What are the advantages of completing Steps 1-5 before Step 6?

resources will we need?

*   What resources are we dedicating to the professional learning?

*   What is our timeline for full implementation by all faculty members?

*   What benchmarks along the way will help us know if we are successful?

*   Are we willing to commit time, energy, and financial resources to this effort for the long term?

*   How will we align this new initiative with existing efforts? What might we need to eliminate to make resources available for this program?

*   How closely do the goals of the professional learning align with our school's improvement goals and the district's strategic goals?

*   How will we assess how the program is initiated, implemented, and sustained?

Planning evaluation at the same time as planning implementation of the professional learning leads to a higher-quality evaluation. Considering both the pro-

gram and evaluation at the same time allows planners to identify what important baseline data to collect, data which may be necessary for demonstrating the professional learning impact.

When planning to evaluate a professional development program, leaders:

1. Assess the design to determine if the staff development program is thorough, well-conceived, and able to be implemented;

2. Identify key questions they hope to answer; and

3. Design the evaluation framework — the plan for conducting the evaluation.

An evaluation framework includes identifying what data will be collected, sources of that data, who will conduct the evaluation, and a timeline (Killion, 2007). Plans should include both formative and summative evaluations. A formative assessment allows professional development leaders to know how well the program is being implemented, provides opportunities to take corrective actions, and answers questions including:

- Are the program activities being implemented as planned?
- Are resources adequate to implement the program as planned?
- To what degree are differences occurring in implementation that may influence the program's results?

A summative evaluation allows professional development leaders to know what impact the program has had and answers questions including:

- Has the learning achieved the intended results?
- What changes for teachers have resulted from the professional learning?
- What changes for students have resulted from the professional learning?
- What changes in the organization have resulted from the professional learning?

Planning the program and evaluation simultaneously gives professional development leaders and the evaluator greater clarity about how the professional learning is intended to work, increasing the likelihood that professional learning will be implemented as designed and that the intended results will be realized.

Step 7: IMPLEMENT, SUSTAIN, AND EVALUATE THE PROFESSIONAL DEVELOPMENT INTERVENTION.

Any new professional development intervention requires constant nurturing and support for it to be implemented at a high level. Staff development leaders, including the principal and teacher leaders, are primarily responsible for monitoring and making adjustments to ensure the initiative's success.

Those responsible for implementation first need a clear understanding of what high-quality performance means and looks like. One tool for reaching agreement on an acceptable level of implementation is an Innovation Configuration (IC) map. IC maps describe and define the essential features of new practice (Hall & Hord, 2001). **Tool 9.8** on the CD describes the components of an Innovation Configuration map as well as strategies for designing your own.

Setting expectations and standards for acceptable implementation will make a significant difference in the quality of implementation. Then use both formative and summative evaluation processes to provide the best data to continually improve professional learning and increase the likelihood that it will achieve the results it was designed to achieve. Formative assessments provide data that can be used to continually adjust and refine the program to strengthen results. Summative evaluation provides information about the impact of professional learning and offers valuable data to improve its results. More information about evaluating professional learning is provided in Chapter 14.

REFERENCES

Easton, L.B. (Ed.) (2008). *Powerful designs for professional learning* (2nd ed.). Oxford, OH: NSDC.

Hall, G. & Hord, S. (2001). *Implementing change: Patterns, principles, and potholes.* Boston: Allyn & Bacon.

Killion, J. (1999). *What works in the middle: Results-based staff development.* Oxford, OH: NSDC.

Killion, J. (2002a). *What works in the elementary school: Results-based staff development.* Oxford, OH: NSDC & NEA.

Killion, J. (2002b). *What works in the high school: Results-based staff development.* Oxford, OH: NSDC & NEA.

Killion, J. (2007). *Assessing impact: Evaluating staff development.* Oxford, OH: NSDC.

TOOL INDEX

TOOL	TITLE	USE
9.1	The numbers game	Tool 9.1 describes skills and strategies useful for analyzing student learning data and identifying student learning needs.
9.2	Taking data to new depths	Tool 9.2 provides information about how teams of teachers can use student data to determine improvement goals.
9.3	Work smarter, not harder	Tool 9.3 is an NSDC newsletter that describes the components of a SMART goal, provides examples, and includes a tree diagram to help in developing SMART goals.
9.4	Heroic efforts: Maintain a focus on priorities	Tool 9.4 focuses on the importance of identifying a small number of priority goals.
9.5	Extreme makeover: Needs assessment edition	Tool 9.5 explains why the typical needs assessment survey does not truly assess educator learning needs. This article can be used to start discussion among administrators and professional development committee members about alternative ways to collect evidence of educator needs.
9.6	Probing for causes	Tool 9.6 describes a process for getting at root causes of learning problems rather than just addressing symptoms.
9.7	Professional development program review	Tool 9.7 provides a framework for collecting information about programs and comparing programs before selecting and implementing one. The completed worksheet is a handy reference guide for each program being considered.
9.8	Clarify your vision with an Innovation Configuration map	Tool 9.8 provides information about creating an Innovation Configuration for a writing program in Arizona. It also includes worksheets and tips about developing an Innovation Configuration map for your own program.
9.9	Our work done well is like the perfect pitch	Tool 9.9 summarizes a six-step process for planning results-based professional learning. It also includes a survey to help schools and districts identify professional learning strengths and needs.

Chapter 10

USING
data

WHERE ARE WE NOW?

In our school, we use data to drive decisions at both the school and classroom levels.

| STRONGLY AGREE | AGREE | NO OPINION | DISAGREE | STRONGLY DISAGREE |

Teachers use data almost daily to assess where students are in the learning continuum.

| STRONGLY AGREE | AGREE | NO OPINION | DISAGREE | STRONGLY DISAGREE |

Data management systems make data easily accessible to teachers.

| STRONGLY AGREE | AGREE | NO OPINION | DISAGREE | STRONGLY DISAGREE |

Our school's culture supports open discussion about student academic performance.

| STRONGLY AGREE | AGREE | NO OPINION | DISAGREE | STRONGLY DISAGREE |

Data are displayed throughout the school in classrooms, offices, and faculty rooms.

| STRONGLY AGREE | AGREE | NO OPINION | DISAGREE | STRONGLY DISAGREE |

A common contention is that educators are data rich and information poor. This is increasingly true since the advent of the No Child Left Behind Act. Data abound. Only slowly are educators beginning to turn data into useful information for making informed decisions.

Conducting a data analysis as a team helps teachers understand problem areas to target and helps them identify possible reasons for the problem.

For example, a team of 4th-grade teachers analyzes district writing samples and state language arts assessments and finds that student organizational skills are weak. They decide to develop their own understanding of writing organization and to apply what they learn to designing three lessons to develop student organization skills before the next writing assessment. World history teachers analyze student essays and are disappointed that their students' work fails to demonstrate critical thinking. They decide that students would benefit from more explicit instruction in critical thinking. As a team, they identify four critical thinking skills, study how to teach those skills to high school students, and use lesson study to develop and refine a model lesson. A group of algebra teachers meets to review semester exam results and discovers that more than half of the students missed the same series of questions. After discussing the possible causes of this pattern, teachers decide that the method they used to assess the skill was different from the way it was presented in the textbook. They study the pros and cons of various methods of assessing the particular skills and determine how they want students to demonstrate an understanding of that particular skill.

Using data effectively requires several competencies. The first is knowing what data exist in the school or district and how to access that data. Principals, teacher leaders, and district staff can help schoolwide teams or individual teams develop this competency. A second competency is analyzing the data. Some schools and districts hold data conferences or data days to guide staff members through the process while simultaneously developing their analysis skills. The third competency is

> **Examining data about student learning is the initial step in identifying the focus of a team's work.**

using data routinely. Data can be used to set instructional goals, to pinpoint areas for improvement, to guide instruction, to set standards for success, and to identify indicators of progress.

In *Using Data/Getting Results: A Practical Guide for School Improvement in Mathematics and Science* (Christopher-Gordon, 2002), Nancy Love identifies 10 reasons for analyzing data. By using data analysis to drive decisions about what they are learning and implementing in their classrooms, teachers can:

- Uncover problems that might otherwise remain invisible;
- Convince people of the need for change;
- Confirm or discredit assumptions about students and school practices;
- Get to the root cause of problems, pinpoint areas where change is most needed, and guide resource allocation;
- Help schools evaluate program effectiveness and keep the focus on student achievement;
- Provide the feedback teachers and administrators need to stay on course;
- Prevent overreliance on standardized tests;
- Prevent one-size-fits-all, quick-fix solutions;
- Enable schools to respond to accountability questions; and
- Help build a culture of inquiry and continuous improvement (2002, pp. 28-30).

Before teams begin their work, they need to determine what the work is. Examining data about student learning is the initial step in identifying the focus of a team's work.

TYPES OF DATA

Working collaboratively to improve teaching and learning, teams identify the specific area of student learning they want to work on. Letting data drive decisions about the focus of a team's learning and work al-

lows both to be more focused on students' specific needs. Teachers have access to a variety of data to use as they identify the main focus for their collaborative work.

Victoria Bernhardt (2004, pp. 16-17) identifies four categories of data that provide valuable information to help school teams understand student learners and the school context.

1. Perception data help teachers develop an understanding of "what students, parents, teachers, and others think about the learning environment."

2. Demographic data "provide descriptive information about the school community — enrollment, attendance, grade level, ethnicity, gender, native language."

3. Student learning data "describe the results of our educational system in terms of standardized test results, grade point averages, standards assessments, and authentic assessments."

4. School processes data "define what teachers are doing to get the results they are getting."

To be more informed about what data exist for teams to use in their own analysis, school faculty may work together as a whole to complete **Tool 10.2**, identifying and categorizing the types of data available to them according to Bernhardt's categories.

DATA ANALYSIS PROCESS

Most data analysis includes these 11 steps:

1. Gather data.
2. Analyze the data.
3. Summarize the analysis.
4. Brainstorm possible causes.
5. Collect additional data.
6. Analyze and interpret the additional data.
7. Identify a goal for student improvement.
8. Determine a course of action.
9. Take action.

10. Collect data.
11. Repeat the process.

1. Gather data.

Teachers typically have access to multiple types of data. When teams are ready to gather data, they may want to determine in advance what kind(s) of data are most appropriate to examine. **Tools 10.1, 10.2**, and **10.3** can help guide their decisions. Teachers continuously examine the results of informal and/or common assessments that they design and administer in their own classrooms. They may also examine results from state assessments, norm-referenced tests, or other forms of formal assessments once a year.

By planning what data to examine, team members can prepare for the next meeting. They can determine who is responsible for gathering and bringing the data to the meeting, copying it for each member, and what protocol to use to examine the data.

The more data a team has, the easier the data analysis process will be.

2. Analyze the data.

Modern and sophisticated data management systems have made data more available in schools. However, unanalyzed data have little meaning. Data analysis is the process of reviewing, studying, examining, and probing the data in order to find patterns, anomalies, and trends. Only by studying data can teachers find information they need to improve their practice and results. When teachers use a process or protocol that offers some structure for looking at data, they discover both strengths and areas for improvement, information they can turn into areas of focused change to improve results for their students.

When collaborative professional learning teams are involved in analyzing data, teachers' multiple perspectives enrich the discoveries. **Tools 10.4** and **10.5** offer

sets of questions that guide teachers in examining data. A structured analysis is more likely to be thorough and complete, resulting in team members identifying:

- Specific areas of deficit;
- What knowledge and skills students need to be able to overcome the deficit;
- Specific students or groups of students for whom the deficit is most prevalent or pronounced; and
- Possible root causes of identified problems.

After teams analyze the data, they can display the information in a way that will make it easy to explain to others and to monitor progress. For example, charts, tables, or other data displays provide quick and easy overviews. Post and use the displays as a reference for ongoing decision making.

3. Summarize the analysis.

Once teams analyze the data, they often want to present their discoveries to other teams. **Tool 10.6** will help teams develop clear, concise statements to communicate.

4. Brainstorm possible causes.

Finding the patterns, anomalies, and trends within the data is not enough. Educators must decide what actions to take to address the target issues by considering the causes behind the data results. Teams' next step is to select a finding to target and search for possible causes, then develop interventions. Possible causes for poor showings in the data can include curriculum, instruction, resources, assessment, or external factors. **Tool 10.7** is useful for brainstorming, categorizing, and deciding possible causes.

At this point in the process, it is important to categorize the causes and narrow them to concentrate only on those where teachers have the greatest leverage to make a difference. Since teachers cannot control most external factors, they should not address them when they are setting goals. If teachers focus on decisions they routinely make, they will be empowered to act rather than feel victimized by circumstances beyond their sphere of control (e.g. low parental involvement).

5. Collect additional data.

To determine a root cause, form and test a hypothesis. If teachers think excessive absence is a reason students fail, gather data to prove or disprove the hypothesis. If students with excessive absences are performing well, then the hypothesis is false. Continue this process until team members believe they understand the possible root causes that are within their sphere of influence and can design a plan to address those. Maintain a log of hypotheses, the data used to verify the hypotheses, and conclusions. **Tool 10.8** is a record-keeping template to help teams with this work.

6. Analyze and interpret the additional data.

Teams that needed additional data to confirm or disprove their hypotheses next repeat steps by analyzing and summarizing the new data. When team members are confident they have discovered the root cause, they can move to the next step.

7. Identify a goal for student improvement.

Once the team has identified possible causes, members set a measurable goal for improvement. Goals that are measurable, set within a specific timeframe, and focused on desired results are helpful to focus action planning. SMART goals (specific, measurable, attainable, results-oriented, time-bound), another quality management tool, help team members set precise targets for their work.

Teams sometimes set short-term goals rather than year-long or multiyear goals. Short-term goals specify what teams will focus on in a more immediate timeframe. For example:

SAMPLE SMART GOALS FOR TEAMS

- Reading scores of 11th-grade males will improve a minimum of two grade levels on the Gates-McGinitie test as a result of participating in the reading lab program during the 2009-10 school year.
- Students scoring below basic on the 2009 math problem-solving items of the state assessment will move to proficient by 2011.
- The number of students enrolled in advanced-level core academic courses in 11th and 12th grades will increase by 15% each year for the next three years.
- The percentage of female, underrepresented, and high-poverty students enrolled in math and science classes will increase by 20% each year for the next three years.

- All students will improve problem-solving by understanding different problem-solving techniques, selecting the most appropriate one, and solving problems at proficient or above on the six-week benchmark assessment.
- 100% of the students will improve their performance by at least one category (from 1 to 2; 2 to 3; 3 to 4) on the quarterly writing assessment in organization and voice.

8. Determine a course of action.

Having a goal focuses the team on actions to accomplish the goal; however, the goal does not define those actions. To move a goal to an action plan, a team lays out specific steps it will take to accomplish its goal. For example, if a team's goal is to improve student performance in reading informational text by 10% overall in one year as measured by the state reading test, members need to know why that goal has not been achieved to know where to concentrate their effort. After researching and considering alternatives, the team decides it wants to increase explicit instruction in informational text. Members decide to take three actions. First, they will learn more about teaching informational text, particularly text structures. Second, they will work with the whole school to identify which text structures will be emphasized in which grades. Finally, they will design and implement lessons, assessments, and assignments for all content areas that integrate explicit instruction on informational text.

9. Take action.

With a plan in place, the team acts on it, adjusting it as needed to produce the greatest results for students. The plan guides team members' actions, serving as a road map for their work.

As a document everyone uses, the plan keeps the focus on the goal and the steps clearly visible for anyone who wants to know what the team is doing. By having a clear plan laid out, team members can review their plan based on their results and determine how to improve their actions if they do not produce the intended results.

10. Collect data.

While implementing the plan, team members use every opportunity to gather data to determine whether they are making progress.

Their best measure of progress is some form of student assessment that provides evidence of whether students are learning to read and interpret informational text in all content areas. Other useful indicators are students' engagement in lessons on informational text or completion rate for assignments. Sometimes just asking students to share what they know now about informa-

tional text is an indicator. Teachers' radars are alert to subtle and substantive changes in how students perform using informational text. Teams can analyze data collected informally at first and then formally on some form of benchmark assessment to lead them to their next goal.

11. Repeat the process.

Repeat the data analysis process several times during a school year. Usually a faculty engages at least once a year in schoolwide data analysis using available high stakes assessment data. Schoolwide data analysis leads to school goals. Teams then repeat the process using student data to identify team goals several times a year.

Not all data analysis is equally effective. Distinguishing data analysis that produces the information necessary for teams to focus their action to be able to achieve clear goals has three characteristics: frequency of data analysis; use of data dialogues; and balancing data sources.

FREQUENCY OF DATA ANALYSIS

Some schools have adopted routines in which teachers analyze data once or twice a year. For data to have a demonstrably strong effect on student learning, teams must engage in data analysis multiple times in a single school year. Annual data from high-stakes assessments is only one source of data about student success.

Teams of teachers will find that they use data more if they plan for data collection and analysis on a more frequent basis. Teams should collectively analyze data at least each marking period and perhaps more frequently. Individual teachers, however, are engaged in using data on almost a daily basis as they assess student learning in their classrooms.

DATA DIALOGUES

School teams use frequent data dialogues to reflect

REFLECTIONS

1. How can we strengthen our use of data to ensure that we are getting the most from the time we invest in data analysis?

2. What barriers do we face in analyzing data that make it challenging for teachers to use data as much as they would like? What can be done to eliminate some of these barriers? What goals do we want to set about removing these barriers?

3. Who on the staff is responsible for helping teachers new to our school develop competence with our data system?

4. What data do we not have that would help us make better decisions about teaching and student learning? How might we get those data? What barriers to getting the data might we anticipate?

5. Name a few incidents in which data provided insights that the team otherwise would not have had. What did we learn in these situations?

on their practice. Different forms of data dialogues are used for different teams and for different purposes. **Table 10.1** summarizes different forms of data dialogues, the kind of data used in each, who is involved, topics for the dialogue, and the frequency of each. **Tool 10.9** describes types of data dialogue useful for whole-school or team-based data dialogues.

BALANCING DATA SOURCES

Looking continuously at the same kind of data may not provide any new insight into student learning, so teachers vary the types and kind of data they look at to expand their understanding of their students. To determine what type of data to use, members consider the goal the team established. For example, the SMART goal examples specified the measure or data source to be used, yet the team might examine other data sources to provide evidence of progress toward the goal. **Table**

10.2 suggests additional, related data sources for each goal. **Tool 10.10** offers other resources on balancing data sources.

Data provide a wealth of information for teachers about student learning, yet simply having the data is insufficient. Teams that want to improve teaching and student learning take time in nearly every meeting to use data to focus their own learning and their collaborative work.

REFERENCES

Bernhardt, V. (2004). *Data analysis for continuous school improvement.* Larchmont, NY: Eye on Education.

Harrison, C. & Bryan, C. (2008). Data dialogue. *JSD, 29*(4), 15-19.

Love, N. (2002). *Using data/getting results: A practical guide for school improvement in mathematics and science.* Norwood, MA: Christopher-Gordon.

Table 10.1 TYPES OF DATA CONVERSATIONS

Type of data dialogue	Data used	Who is involved	Conversation topics	Frequency
Whole-school conversations	State assessments, district benchmarks	School improvement team, entire staff	• Patterns of student achievement • Needs for schoolwide programs (instructional, curricular, professional learning) • Needs for additional knowledge and skills for staff	2 times a year
One-on-one conversations with focus on multiyear growth of students	State assessments, benchmark exams, end-of-course assessments, classroom assessments, common assessments	Teacher and administrator and/or coach	• Growth of students • Overall proficiency of students • Instructional strategies to meet student learning needs	2 to 3 times a year
Department and/or grade-level teams with focus on individual student interventions	Student performance on classroom and common assessments, discipline records, student work	Core teams, grade-level teams	• Diagnosis of individual knowledge and skills • Next steps for students • Grouping of students for instruction and intervention • Pyramid of interventions	Once a month or more often
Department and/or grade-level teams with focus on instructional strategies	State assessments, benchmark assessments, common assessments, unit assessments	Grade-level or content-area groups	• Growth of students • Patterns in proficiency • Instructional strategies • Assessment strategies	Once a week to once every 6 to 8 weeks
Student goal-setting conversations	Student work, grades, state assessments, common assessments, benchmark assessments	Teacher and individual students	• Goal setting • Strategies for success • Celebrations of learning	Once a week to once a month

Source: Harrison, C. & Bryan, C. (2008). Data Dialogue. *JSD, 29*(4), 15-19.

Table 10.2 SMART GOALS

SMART goal	Designated data sources	Related data sources
Reading scores of 11th-grade males will improve a minimum of two grade levels on the Gates-McGinitie test as a result of participating in the reading lab program during the 2009-10 school year.	Gates-McGinitie reading test scores	• Classroom comprehension assessment scores • Classroom task using reading skills
Students scoring below basic on the 2009 math problem-solving items of the state assessment will score proficient by 2011.	State math assessment	• Benchmark assessments • End-of-course assessments • Performance tasks in math • Performance tasks in science that depend on math • Math journals
The number of students enrolled in advanced-level core academic courses in 11th and 12th grades will increase by 15% each year for the next three years.	Class enrollment records	• Interviews with students qualified to enroll in advanced-level courses who did not • Student surveys about their post-graduation plans • Grades • Grade distributions
The percentage of female, underrepresented, and high-poverty students enrolled in math and science classes will increase by 20% each year for the next three years.	Class enrollment records	• Focus groups with target student groups • Grade distributions • Grades • Interview with counselors • Drop-out data
All students will improve their problem solving by understanding different problem-solving techniques, selecting the most appropriate one, and solving problems at proficient level or above on the six-week benchmark assessment.	Benchmark assessment	• Problem of the week • Daily problem-solving tasks
100% of students will improve their performance by at least one category (from 1 to 2; 2 to 3; 3 to 4) on the quarterly writing assessment in organization and voice.	Quarterly writing assessment	• Writing portfolio • Weekly journal review

TOOL INDEX

TOOL	TITLE	USE
10.1	Data use reflection guide	Tool 10.1 is a reflection tool for individuals, teams, and full school faculties to use to identify the data they most often use.
10.2	Types of data available	Tool 10.2 is used by the full school faculty or school leadership team to identify the types of data readily available within the school.
10.3	Student data checklist	Tool 10.3 guides teams and school faculties to identify various forms of student demographic data.
10.4	Data analysis protocol (informal)	Tool 10.4 is an informal data analysis protocol for teams or faculties to use to look at a common set of classroom-generated data.
10.5	Data analysis protocol (formal)	Tool 10.5 is a more formal and specific data analysis protocol to use to look at annual student assessment data, end-of-course assessments, or other high-stakes assessments.
10.6	Crafting data summary statements	Tool 10.6 guides teams or whole faculties in writing summary statements drawn from the data analysis process as a way of synthesizing the data analysis process.
10.7	Fishbone diagram	Tool 10.7 is a tool for organizing possible causes for particular observations drawn from data. The tool helps teams cluster their ideas into categories.
10.8	Hypothesis-testing record-keeping sheet	Tool 10.8 helps teams record their hypotheses about root causes and their conclusions about their findings from further data analysis related to each hypothesis.
10.9	Data dialogue	Tool 10.9 is an article that describes a variety of data dialogues useful for teams and whole faculties.
10.10	Striking a balance	Tool 10.10 is an article that describes how one district implemented benchmark assessments. A useful table describes assessments that are sources of data for districts, schools, and teams.

Chapter 11

DESIGNS
for professional learning

WHERE ARE WE NOW?

Teachers in our school work collaboratively on most tasks related to teaching and learning.

STRONGLY AGREE   AGREE   NO OPINION   DISAGREE   STRONGLY DISAGREE

In our school, professional learning is typically a whole-school experience.

STRONGLY AGREE   AGREE   NO OPINION   DISAGREE   STRONGLY DISAGREE

Most teacher professional learning occurs during the school day and year.

STRONGLY AGREE   AGREE   NO OPINION   DISAGREE   STRONGLY DISAGREE

Teachers determine the focus of their professional learning.

STRONGLY AGREE   AGREE   NO OPINION   DISAGREE   STRONGLY DISAGREE

Teachers choose how they will design their collaborative professional learning.

STRONGLY AGREE   AGREE   NO OPINION   DISAGREE   STRONGLY DISAGREE

Teachers who collaborate to refine their practice and improve student learning find that collaborative learning can be rewarding and productive, as well as informative and enriching. However, collaborative learning and work also can be messy and challenging. Team members need to make decisions about how best to work together and to use their collaborative time. When teachers know of multiple designs for using their collaborative time to meet agreed-upon goals, they are far more likely to use the time effectively.

Effective teamwork requires numerous decisions. Some decisions depend on what the team wants to accomplish and others on how the team learns. The first decision teams make is how they will learn, whether outside-in, inside-out, or some combination.

Outside-in learning

Outside-in professional development means someone from outside the school serves as the external assistance provider to help teachers learn instructional strategies to use in their classrooms — for example,

how to teach students to write persuasive text. The outside expert is available, affordable, and willing to help teachers learn the new strategy. This individual might be a central office staff member from the curriculum or professional development department or a consultant. Not all external experts help teachers learn both the content they are teaching and the content-specific pedagogy.

A common approach to outside-in learning is having teachers leave school to gain knowledge and skill and bring that knowledge back. Teachers might participate in workshops at the district office, after school, at regional agencies, or through local college or university courses or summer programs. This form of learning has limited impact on the school as a whole because teachers usually participate alone or in small teams. The assumption that a few teachers' learning spreads throughout the school rarely is realized.

Outside-in is a more common, traditional, and often formal method for teacher learning. Most teachers have extensive experience with this type of professional development because it has been practiced in schools for a long time. This form of learning does not generally result in deep changes in teaching or student learning. Another option is available.

Inside-out learning

Inside-out learning is less formal and allows teachers to collaborate within their school buildings. Educators less familiar with or less experienced in this form of professional learning often wonder how it can replace traditional professional development. In fact, critics have described the process as "shared ignorance" when the collaboration is uninformed and perpetuates the status quo. Yet collaborative professional learning among teachers, as described in Chapter 1, includes deepening teachers' content knowledge and refining instructional practice, changes that do not occur in all professional learning communities.

When teachers work in collaborative professional learning teams within their own schools, they set goals that are specific to their own and their students' learning needs, then craft an action plan to accomplish those goals. Action plans define the content of professional learning, answering the question, "What do teachers need to know and do for students to achieve the established goals?", and the process for learning, answering the question, "How will we as a team design our collaborative learning to meet our goals?" Teachers then explore various designs to determine how they will learn. When teachers have not experienced informal or self-directed forms of professional learning, they often ask for more traditional forms of learning or fail to bring new information, skills, strategies, or practices into their practice. Collaborative professional learning includes opportunities for teachers to try various designs for professional learning and to select designs appropriate for achieving their learning goals.

School-based collaborative professional learning is part of a comprehensive professional development program. While learning in teams is the largest portion, collaborative professional learning is supplemented with learning from experts, participation in conferences, and other forms of more formal professional development. Teams choose from the array of learning strategies to help them accomplish their goals expeditiously.

These designs for collaborative professional learning allow teachers to deepen their content knowledge and expand their repertoire of content-specific instructional strategies.

DETERMINE STUDENT LEARNING

Many districts and states have developed resources to help teachers and curriculum developers identify the content knowledge and skills students in each grade and course are expected to learn. A learning team's primary function is to determine what students are expected to learn. Members review, study, and analyze content standards and the district curriculum to identify essential student learning. **Tool 11.1** on the CD outlines a process for determining the specific content and skills embedded within the standards. With this information and assessments of students' current understanding, teachers can decide what to teach, in what sequence, and to what depth and scope.

USE COMMON ASSESSMENTS

Common assessments are tools that teachers develop together to assess student learning. Teachers use common assessments to be consistent in how they deliver the curriculum and what they expect students to learn.

Teachers can learn a great deal by developing, administering, and scoring common assessments. They learn, for example, to calibrate their expectations to those of others teaching the same grade or course. They learn how other teachers assess student learning, and they can compare others' methods to their own processes. They learn which aspects of a concept other teachers stress and how much. By developing common assessments, teachers clarify their expectations for students, determine what good work looks like, clarify their understanding of the standards, and expand their assessment literacy.

Teachers in cross-grade level or course teams can develop common assessments to use frequently or periodically throughout the school year. For example, algebra teachers might invite geometry teachers to develop a common final examination for all algebra classes since most students would take geometry next. Fifth-grade teachers might work together to develop social studies common assessments. Teachers of world languages might meet with partners in other district schools to develop common semester and final exams.

The first step in the process is developing the assessment. **Tool 11.2** on the CD will help teams think about some critical decisions teachers make when they construct classroom assessments. An article by Jay McTighe and Marcella Emberger (**Tool 11.3** on the CD) offers several ideas for how to collaborate to develop assessments.

The next step is administering the assessment. Teachers should agree on a time frame in which students will complete assessments and on the teacher's role in the assessment, as well as what accommodations will be made for students who require them. When teachers have agreed on these points, they give the assessment.

The third step is scoring. Teachers score assessments on their own, in a team meeting, or with other team members. When teachers are able to score one another's assessments or score assessments together, they develop a deeper understanding of student learning. One recommendation is to have each team member bring several completed assessments to a team meeting and to score them as a group, using a common rubric or scoring guide. Teachers then are able to adjust or

Table 11.1 STAGES OF TEAM DEVELOPMENT BY SAFETY AND STRUCTURE LEVELS

Stage of development	Recommended safety level	Recommended structure level
Forming	High	High
Storming/ norming	High	Mid
Performing	Low	Low

modify the scoring guide before they score every student's work, and they can calibrate their scoring so students have consistency.

The last and most important step is to review assessment results and make instructional and curriculum decisions based on the data. For example, if teachers find that a high percentage of students missed a key concept, they can plan together how to reteach the concept or how to give students more practice with the concept. If teachers find that one teacher's students outperformed another's, they can talk about the instructional processes and resources the teacher in the higher-performing class used, identify what they believe contributed to student success, and plan how all teachers will integrate the successful strategies in their classrooms.

Collaborative professional learning teams can center their work on multiple cycles of developing assessments, scoring them, and making instructional decisions based on the results.

EXAMINE STUDENT WORK

Examining student work helps teachers better understand what students learned and how to calibrate their expectations of students for greater consistency classroom to classroom. Teachers can learn a tremendous amount by looking at students' work product and

Table 11.2 PROFESSIONAL DESIGNS BY SAFETY AND STRUCTURE LEVELS

Designs for professional learning	Recommended safety level	Recommended structure level
Peeling an onion	High	Mid
Common assessments	Mid	Mid
Success analysis protocol	Mid	Mid
Descriptive review process	High	High
Collaborative assessment conference	Mid	High
Action research	Mid	Mid
Lesson study	Low	Mid
Say something	High	Mid
Author assumptions	Mid	High

at the teacher's assignment that generated the work. **Tool 11.4** on the CD is a brief article that gives an overview of the process.

Generally, teachers bring one or more samples of student work to the group, and the group discusses the samples using a protocol or discussion guide. As teachers examine students' work, they deepen their understanding of how students learn, how their colleagues structure learning assignments, and which students are succeeding.

The protocols in **Tools 11.5, 11.6,** and **11.7** on the CD are included for examining student work, with each taking the process progressively deeper. These processes are a starting point for teams with little or no experience working together and building a collaborative culture. Team members can add more complex protocols that call for critical feedback after they are comfortable with one another and with sharing their own and students' work publicly.

Teams should carefully consider when to use various learning designs to ensure members feel comfortable in the collaborative process. When staff are new to collaborative professional learning, designs that have greater structure, explicit expectations of and processes for team members offer more personal and professional comfort for team members because they are likely to be less intrusive into teachers' practice. When a school's culture supports collaboration and teachers are more familiar with teaming, teachers might select designs that focus more on teaching practices.

In addition to members' level of comfort with collaboration, a team's stage of development matters. If a team is in the forming stage, it is better to use more structured designs for professional learning to offer members a greater sense of safety. When a team progresses through the stages of team development, members are more likely to choose designs that challenge their assumptions and practices. **Table 11.1** summarizes stages of team development and the safety and structure levels recommended for each stage. **Table 11.2** summarizes the safety and structure levels of learning designs and protocols included on the CD.

Whether or not a team is new to collaborative learning and work, teachers have the majority voice in designing their learning processes. Coaches and principals may offer advice or guidance. Teachers, though, are ultimately responsible for their learning and have the final decision.

Designs of professional learning include action re-

REFLECTIONS

1. What characteristics of effective professional learning experiences are most meaningful for our team's members?

2. How has professional learning been designed in the past, more outside-in or inside-out? How effective have these learning experiences been in changing teaching and student learning?

3. What assumptions do school administrators and teachers have about teachers' ability to choose their own designs for professional learning?

4. How will the school leadership team help teachers learn about various designs for professional learning?

5. Of the designs described in this chapter, which are most appropriate for accomplishing our team's learning goals? Which are inappropriate? Explain why.

search, peer coaching, lesson study text-rendering protocols, book studies, case discussions, co-teaching, model teaching, examining student work, portfolios, and other options. The tools for this chapter on the CD include several designs.

CONDUCT ACTION RESEARCH

Action research is another collaborative learning process that supports teachers in learning from their own work. Teachers design and conduct a systematic research study of their work in their own classrooms and schools. They outline questions, gather and analyze data, then reach conclusions based on their work. Action research allows teachers to examine the impact of their teaching practices and to understand how context influences the results they achieve. Action research is especially powerful when a team of teachers gathers data about the same or related questions and combines data to create a cross-classroom research study. **Tool 11.8** outlines the action research process and provides tools for conducting action research in the classroom.

LESSON STUDY

Lesson study is yet another powerful form of collaborative learning. In lesson study, teachers collabora-

tively design a lesson, observe a team member teaching that lesson, debrief, and revise the lesson based on their observations. Lesson study makes public the work teachers do each day in isolation. Through the lesson study process, teachers develop a deeper understanding of content and pedagogy. They gain new understanding about how students learn and about how their instructional decisions influence student success. **Tool 11.9** provides useful resources to assist teachers with conducting lesson studies.

OVERVIEW OF DESIGNS

Tool 11.12 is an overview of designs for professional learning described in *Powerful Designs for Professional Learning* (Easton, 2008). Many of the designs are appropriate for collaborative professional learning teams. Teams that know how to structure their time, choose designs appropriate to their learning goals, and use a variety of designs over time are more satisfied and productive.

REFERENCE

Easton, L.B. (Ed.). (2008). *Powerful designs for professional learning* (2nd ed.). Oxford, OH: NSDC.

TOOL INDEX

TOOL	TITLE	USE
11.1	Peeling a standard	Tool 11.1 helps a team dissect a content standard to identify the grade or course-specific knowledge and skills to guide instruction and assessment decisions.
11.2	Common assessment planning tool	Tool 11.2 guides teams to develop common or benchmark assessments to align with the content and skills students are expected to learn.
11.3	Teamwork on assessments creates powerful professional development	Tool 11.3 provides background information on the benefits of developing common assessments and recommends strategies.
11.4	Group wise: Strategies for examining student work together	Tool 11.4 is an overview of the decisions a team makes when examining student work.
11.5	Success analysis protocol	Tool 11.5 is a protocol for identifying and sharing successful practices.
11.6	Descriptive review protocol	Tool 11.6 is a protocol for looking at student work by identifying what students do well.
11.7	Collaborative assessment conference	Tool 11.7 is a protocol for looking at student work, finding what the work reveals about the student, and exploring classroom practices leading to the student's work.
11.8	Teacher research leads to learning, action	Tool 11.8 is an article that includes strategies for conducting action research.
11.9	Lesson study	Tool 11.9 is an article that includes strategies for conducting lesson study.
11.10	Say something protocol	Tool 11.10 is a protocol that engages readers in pairs or small teams with text as they read. It is useful if team members will be reading at the meeting in order to use text to inform their work.
11.11	Author assumptions	Tool 11.11 is used to uncover an author's assumptions and deepen a reader's understanding of the text. It allows the reader to make more informed interpretations or judgments about the text.
11.12	Process: Selecting the design that works with context and content	Tool 11.12 is an overview of various designs for professional learning and criteria for selecting designs.

Chapter 12

FACILITATING
collaborative professional learning teams

WHERE ARE WE NOW?

Teams in our school know the stages of team development and can identify which stage they are in.

STRONGLY AGREE   AGREE   NO OPINION   DISAGREE   STRONGLY DISAGREE

Teachers in our school are more comfortable working in teams than independently.

STRONGLY AGREE   AGREE   NO OPINION   DISAGREE   STRONGLY DISAGREE

Our school faculty has established agreements about how staff members treat one another.

STRONGLY AGREE   AGREE   NO OPINION   DISAGREE   STRONGLY DISAGREE

Teachers use structures and processes to make their collaborative learning teams efficient and productive.

STRONGLY AGREE   AGREE   NO OPINION   DISAGREE   STRONGLY DISAGREE

Teams have strategies for resolving conflict that occurs among team members.

STRONGLY AGREE   AGREE   NO OPINION   DISAGREE   STRONGLY DISAGREE

ollaborative professional learning teams do not result from luck or magic but from discipline and commitment. A team is a collection of individuals who commit to working together to accomplish a common goal. Team members choose to share their individual knowledge, talents, and expertise so that the team benefits.

Teams establish systems to ensure that they are productive and effective. They engage in intentional team building and regularly assess their work and their functioning as a team. On a good team, members make the inner workings of the team seem effortless, even while invisible structures and processes are in place to ensure the team operates smoothly. Every member takes personal and collective responsibility for the team's success.

Teams that work collaboratively increase their efficiency and effectiveness by:

- Identifying roles and responsibilities;
- Establishing agreements;
- Sharing leadership;
- Creating and maintaining a sense of team; and

- Understanding stages of team development.

IDENTIFYING ROLES AND RESPONSIBILITIES

To be successful, teams require some structure. One way teams reach success is to determine members' roles and responsibilities. Typical roles include team member, facilitator, recorder, and timekeeper. While other roles can be added, these are the most basic and common.

Team member. A team member is an active part of the collaborative team. Members support the team's work by staying focused on the agenda, purpose, and goal. They actively engage in the team's work and monitor their own behavior(s) so that they adhere to the team's agreements. They help the facilitator and other team members accomplish the work of the team. They recognize that they have a responsibility for the team's success.

Facilitator. A facilitator is responsible for the meeting process. Together with the team, the facilitator sets the agenda and determines what learning design to use to accomplish the team's work. She or he calls the team's meeting to order, ensures agreements are honored, moves the team through the agenda so that all items are addressed as planned, maintains the safety of the team for all members, and helps team members stay focused on the agenda and team success. The facilitator remains neutral so that she or he is open to all perspectives and ensures fairness and equity in team interactions. The facilitator may take the role of team member if necessary, but must clearly state that she or he is stepping out of the facilitator's role to assume the role of team member.

Recorder. The recorder, with team members' help, completes the team meeting log, maintaining the record of team interactions and decisions. The team collectively decides how extensive its record will be. In some cases, the log is a summary of decisions and key points. In other cases, the record includes a more extensive description of the discussion and viewpoints presented. The recorder may opt to serve as both a team member and as recorder if the team is comfortable with this dual role and if she or he can simultaneously record the meeting and participate. The recorder's challenge is to use team members' language and to maintain neutrality in logging the proceedings.

Timekeeper. The timekeeper's role includes informing the team about how its meeting time is progressing. Agenda items may have specific time limits, and the timekeeper gives a signal when time is running out. The team then may decide to table a discussion that can't be finished in the allotted time or to extend the time for a certain item while adjusting time for other agenda items. When teams have worked together for awhile, they become more efficient with time usage; however, the timekeeper's role remains important to ensuring team success.

ESTABLISHING AGREEMENTS

A major factor in any team's success is members'

willingness to take time early on to establish clear agreements about member behavior. Sometimes called norms, these agreements are central to team productivity. All teams have agreements that emerge over time. When teams fail to establish explicit agreements, implicit ones emerge. These agreements can either help or hinder a team's success. According to Daniel Goleman, Richard Boyatzis, and Annie McKee (2002), agreements or norms:

- Provide psychological security within teams that allows team members to feel interpersonal safety;
- Prevent problems that often interfere with a team's ability to be creative and fully functioning;
- Separate a loose collection of individuals from a high-performing team;
- Maximize the team's emotional intelligence;
- Contribute to the team's ability to self-manage; and
- Address two elements of a team's emotional reality: inclusion dynamics, "who's in and who's out" (p. 185) and members' roles, "who does what, and why" (p. 185).

Teams might set up initial agreements in several areas: time, location, communication processes, and structures around members' responsibilities and how decisions will be made. Some sample agreements are:

Time
- The meeting will start and end on time.
- All members will be ready, present, and prepared to initiate their work on time.

Location
- Team members will meet in each other's classrooms on a rotating basis.
- Meetings will be in the library conference room unless otherwise arranged.

Communication
- Team members will listen respectfully to all ideas.
- Team members will balance inquiry (search for understanding) and advocacy (intent to persuade).

STRATEGIES

Dave Ellis of Breakthrough Enterprises (www.fallingawake.com) offers some simple, yet powerful strategies for handling breakdowns within the team. Some tips, adapted from his work (www.fallingawake.com/book/fa/063.pdf):

- Keep agreements. This is quite simple. Keep an agreement as a promise. Promises are intentions to do something. They are not to be taken lightly. Broken promises lead to broken relationships and mistrust.

- When you must break an agreement, acknowledge the transgression in advance. Do whatever is necessary so the broken agreement doesn't interfere with the team's goal or members' relationships, and recommit to keeping the agreement from this point on. While acknowledging a broken agreement in advance is better than not acknowledging it at all, the fact remains that a promise was reneged on. Repeatedly breaking agreements, even with acknowledgment, erodes the team's trust and a person's integrity.

- When you break an agreement without acknowledging it in advance, take the first opportunity to take responsibility for the breakdown. Recommit to the agreement if this is an isolated incident. Renegotiate the agreement if it seems likely it will be more frequent. Agreements should be taken so seriously that if they don't work, the team must find others that do.

Members' responsibilities

- All members will participate.
- Team members are responsible for monitoring their own and one another's adherence to the team's agreements.

Decision making

- We will make all decisions by majority (75%) after all views have been aired.

One of the most challenging issues for a team to handle is broken agreements. Broken agreements are inevitable. Members are human, and they make mistakes. Things happen. Sometimes, without a clear intention, members forget. The sign of a strong team is its ability to handle these breakdowns, learn from them, and move on.

Teams might discuss ways of handling breakdowns before they happen so that when one does occur, it can be handled efficiently and effectively. Facilitators can both model and teach team members how to handle

broken agreements. The facilitator, however, is not the agreement police. All team members share responsibility for upholding the agreements and ensuring their implementation. If keeping to the outlined terms becomes burdensome, the team needs to reassess its agreements and its well-being.

Teams that learn to deal with breakdowns efficiently and effectively can continue their work without resentment, ill feelings, or interruptions. They have processes in place. Agreements are the grease that keeps the team's gears turning smoothly.

Tool 12.1 is a protocol to guide the development of agreements.

SHARING LEADERSHIP

Teams benefit from leadership when they are forming, yet over time leadership evolves to the point where the most sophisticated teams become leaderless and function efficiently and effectively. Early in a team's work, it is helpful to have a strong facilitator who will guide the team through its work. It is also important to simultaneously develop the leadership skills of all teams members so they can share leadership within the team. By sharing knowledge and skills about facilitation with team members, team facilitators are developing leadership capacity, helping a team become more independent, and increasing the likelihood that a team will be successful long into the future. Facilitation skills used in collaborative teams can also be transferred to classrooms so teachers learn important strategies to use with their students, helping students become effective team members, an important life skill.

CREATING AND MAINTAINING A SENSE OF TEAM

When teams first come together, they are merely a collection of individuals who have their own perspectives, frames of reference, and goals. However, as team members work together over time with a clear purpose and with success, they develop a deep sense of interdependence.

To reach that stage, team members benefit from some basic understanding of team development. Carl Glickman, Michael Fullan, Andy Hargreaves, and others describe teams as being a collection of individuals, congenial entities, or collegial work teams. At first, individuals continue to hold their own interests and needs at the forefront. Members' interactions are congenial or polite. Teachers who believe working collaboratively increases their workload or interferes with their productivity are typically still in the individual orientation. Group members who come together and maintain a healthy distance through polite exchanges and then leave and do whatever they wish are congenial entities. These members are noticeable by their courtesy, distance, and aloofness.

Soon, however, interactions shift as members begin

jockeying for recognized leadership or status within the group. When this happens, conflicts emerge. Team members unfamiliar with the stages of team development and unskilled in working collaboratively will simply choose to leave the team because their experience is uncomfortable.

If team members have some skills in resolving differences and persist in working through difficult issues, they will jell and become a genuine team. As they work together, team members develop a shared perspective, experiences, and common goals. Teams that are collegial roll up their sleeves, share their points of view, do not worry about disagreement, and make everyone's work easier. However, the road from individuals to teams is not easily traveled. With some understanding, members can accelerate their team's development by understanding these stages. Bruce Tuckman (1965) identified four stages of team development:

> As team members work together over time with a clear purpose and with success, they develop a deep sense of interdependence.

1. Forming: The first stage of team development occurs when the team forms. It can easily be represented as a group of individuals who come together and who are questioning their place within the team, the team's purpose, their contribution to the team, and their commitment to the team's work.

2. Storming: As members understand their purpose and place, the commitment that will be required, and needed contribution, reality sets in. Team members may experience some disagreement, even conflict, about their individual influence within the team, processes for accomplishing the work, or even beliefs about or the direction of the work. According to Daniel Goleman, Richard Boyatzis, and Annie McKee, "Groups begin to change [be productive] only when they first have fully grasped the reality of how they function, particularly when individuals in the group recognize that they're working in situations that are dissonant or uncomfortable" (2002, p. 172). In some cases, teams in the storming stage lack the support, skills, or persistence to work through disagreements. When they do commit to work through these challenges, they move to the next stage of development.

3. Norming: Although team members establish agreements when they first come together, they may find it helpful after moving to this stage to revisit those agreements, refine them, and extend them to reflect what members learned in the storming stage. The norming stage brings the team together not as a collection of individuals, but as a team with a shared vision, goals, and commitment. Team members begin to recognize the value of working in a team.

> **Conflict is the irritant that shapes the pearl. It is the disequilibrium that brings equilibrium.**

4. Performing: Teams at this stage are highly productive. Members' efforts toward forming a team can now be directed to the team's work. Because there is synergy among team members, they find their work is easier when done collaboratively. They prefer to be in the team because the teamwork is both personally rewarding and highly productive.

Once members have an initial sense of team, an important part of the work is to determine how to maintain the team. To continue developing, teams benefit from feedback about how well they are functioning. Beginning early in the team's work, take a few minutes at the end of each meeting to assess team members' adherence to their agreements. Then, over time, teams may schedule opportunities for feedback. **Tool 12.2** is a survey that might be used to assess team productivity.

A variety of tools included on the CD for this chapter help teams and facilitators work together effectively. The tools provide information on how teams function, how they develop over time, and how to create structures and agreements for productive work.

A WORD ABOUT CONFLICT

Conflict, like broken agreements, is inevitable. Many fear conflict; however, conflict is to be celebrated. Conflict is the irritant that shapes the pearl. It brings possibilities for deeper relationships, new perspectives, appreciation of differences, and clarity of beliefs that shape an individual's and the team's actions. It is the disequilibrium that brings equilibrium.

While most people are so uncomfortable with conflict that they avoid it at all costs, the result is lack of authenticity. Allowing conflict to emerge and working through it holds more promise for moving a team to the next level of development.

These tips for working through conflict can help both the facilitator and teams to feel more comfortable when conflict emerges.

- Let conflict emerge without fear or anxiety.
- Commit to resolving the conflict productively by keeping all parties fully engaged and the team's purpose and goals in the forefront.
- Get clear on what the issues are, not what people want as the solution. For example, rather than discussing whether to work with a new math curriculum or the old math curriculum, discuss what would allow teachers to feel competent in teaching the chosen math curriculum, such as ways to make sure students are getting the best instruction possible, to make sure students perform well on the test, to meet school board and district expectations, to reduce preparation time, to get help in developing new instructional materials, etc.
- Use a creative problem-solving process to resolve conflicts.
- Identify the problem in factual terms. For example, "We have different levels of commitment to imple-

REFLECTIONS

1. What stage of development characterizes most teams in our school? What evidence supports this answer? What strategies do facilitators use to advance team development?

2. As teams mature, they become more productive. Give an example of how this has occurred in a team of which you were a member.

3. How has conflict enhanced or derailed a team you have served on? How did you feel when you realized conflict was inevitable? How did the team handle the conflict?

4. What skills and knowledge do you have to facilitate a team? How are facilitators in your school prepared for this important role? Who supports facilitators to be the best that they can be?

5. Who serves as facilitators of collaborative professional learning teams within your school? How were they identified? What special qualifications are needed to become a team facilitator?

menting the new math curriculum."

- Brainstorm solutions.
- Assess the viability of each solution against the criteria identified.
- Determine the appropriateness of the solutions to the situation at hand.
- Commit to implement the selected solution for a specific period of time.
- Reconvene to examine how well the solution met the criteria and worked.
- Make adjustments as needed.
- Re-evaluate the solution in a designated period of time.

Teams that handle conflict smoothly move to the performing stage of development quickly. They use conflict to deepen their understanding of individual members' perspectives and to enrich their experiences. They tap individual expertise so that all members benefit from the collective expertise they share.

They appreciate conflict for the opportunities and possibilities it holds rather than fear it or hide its existence.

SUCCESSFUL TEAMS

Successful teams make a commitment to their own development. When team members invest energy and time in developing and maintaining their sense of team, they will be more satisfied with their work and produce better work. In *The Wisdom of Crowds* (Random House, 2004), author James Surowiecki asserts that teams are more successful than individuals in making decisions. He cites several examples of how teams, when they pool their individual expertise, perform better than any one individual.

REFERENCES

Goleman, D., Boyatzis, B., & McKee, A. (2002). *Primal leadership: Learning to lead with emotional intelligence.* Boston: Harvard Business School Press.

Surowiecki, J. (2004.) *The wisdom of crowds.* New York: Random House.

Tuckman, B. (1965). Developmental sequence in small groups. *Psychological Bulletin, 63*(6), 384-399.

TOOL INDEX

TOOL	TITLE	USE
12.1	Protocol for developing agreements	Tool 12.1 will guide teams in developing agreements to support their collaborative interactions.
12.2	Building effective teams	Tool 12.2 is a survey to help team members analyze strengths and challenges, plan staff development to address critical issues, and celebrate the team's progress in becoming more effective.
12.3	Transform your group into a team	Tool 12.3 is a newsletter article and survey to use to develop understanding of the stages of team development.
12.4	Which stage is your team in?	Tool 12.4 is a survey to collect members' perceptions of the team's stage of development.
12.5	Becoming a productive team	Tool 12.5 offers suggestions for moving a team from its current stage to the next level.
12.6	Team agreement template	Tool 12.6 is a template teams can use to record their agreements for individual, team, and school reference.
12.7	Articles on conflict resolution in *Tools for Schools* December/January 1999	Tool 12.7 is a set of resources on conflict, including suggestions for resolving conflict, a survey for how individuals handle conflict, a checklist for resolving conflict, and a helpful tool for identifying positions and interests.

Chapter 13

TEAM
planning
and reporting

WHERE ARE WE NOW?

We include time in all schoolwide meetings to discuss what collaborative professional learning teams are doing and learning.

STRONGLY AGREE   AGREE   NO OPINION   DISAGREE   STRONGLY DISAGREE

Structures exist within our school to make it possible for teams to learn from what other teams are studying.

STRONGLY AGREE   AGREE   NO OPINION   DISAGREE   STRONGLY DISAGREE

Our school uses well-defined processes to keep everyone informed about what teachers are learning in their collaborative professional learning teams.

STRONGLY AGREE   AGREE   NO OPINION   DISAGREE   STRONGLY DISAGREE

Teams of teachers (grade-level, resource, interdisciplinary, department, etc.) develop written plans to guide their collaborative professional learning.

STRONGLY AGREE   AGREE   NO OPINION   DISAGREE   STRONGLY DISAGREE

The school's use of collaborative professional learning teams is reflected in district and school professional development plans.

STRONGLY AGREE   AGREE   NO OPINION   DISAGREE   STRONGLY DISAGREE

ollaborative professional learning teams plan their work and regularly report what they are doing and learning to create a schoolwide culture of collaboration. Without planning and reporting, professional learning teams may create a new isolation within a school that Andrew Hargreaves (1998) calls "balkanization." Hargreaves refers to situations in which team members work so closely together that they isolate themselves from the rest of the staff. Some might argue that having teachers who work so closely within the team is better than a school culture of complete individual isolation, competition, or even jealousy; however, balkanization diminishes the faculty's ability to create a schoolwide emphasis on improving teaching and learning and to feel a shared responsibility for student success.

Although each team is an entity, each also is part of a set of teams within the school connected to a common core set of goals and to one another. NSDC's definition of professional development stresses the importance of teachers taking collective responsibility for student achievement, and teams, too, have collective responsibility for the success of other teams. When teams frequently share ideas with other teams, address challenges of collaboration, and highlight the learning that occurs in each, they build a strong culture of collective responsibility for teaching quality and student achievement.

As schools create opportunities for more collaborative professional learning, leaders can establish planning and reporting processes that will increase cross-team collaboration and learning. These processes, when they become routine, contribute to building a schoolwide collaborative culture. Both teams and the principal are responsible for making these processes routine.

TEAM PLANNING

Two methods of planning can help keep the team focused and on the path toward improved teacher and student learning.

Action plans

Once teams analyze student data, set SMART (specific, measurable, attainable, results-oriented, time-bound) goals for professional learning and student learning, and identify possible strategies for collaboration, the next step is to develop a plan of action that helps the team and others know how team members plan to accomplish the goal or goals they identified. A team's action plan is a road map with a timeline that helps members stay on course, make intentional course changes if necessary, and communicate to their publics about their work.

Team action plans include:

- Goal(s)
- Actions (tasks)
- Indicators of accomplishment
- Person(s) responsible (talent)
- Timeline
- Resources requested

The principal receives a copy of each plan and identifies resources each team has requested to determine how to provide those. In addition, the principal may offer the team feedback on its plan and recommend other resources or strategies for members to consider.

Perhaps the most important part of the principal's work is finding commonalities between and among teams' plans. When these commonalities occur, the principal informs each team and encourages teams to share ideas, information, and resources so that they can expand the scope of their learning. Some principals may choose to share each team's list of goals with every faculty member so that all teachers know the focus of every team's work. Individual members of a team should be willing to share their goals with colleagues on other teams and to ask about colleagues' goals as well.

Leaders also can post a copy of the team's plan in the staff lounge or in their meeting room so other teams' members can read and review the plan. Some teachers post their learning team plans on the school's faculty web site or in their professional development management system, or teams may have other forms of online communities to organize and post resources. Teams also may choose to post their logs and updates in the same location. By studying how other teams plan to accom-

plish their work and finding connections between their own team and others, team members extend their learning, resources, and potentially their results.

Meeting agendas

Preparing an agenda for each meeting helps teams stay organized. The team can set the next meeting's agenda before the end of each meeting. An agenda helps team members know how to prepare for each meeting, how the meeting is organized, and what will be accomplished and how. The agenda will be most helpful if it includes the following information:

- Date, time, and location of the meeting;
- Meeting purpose describing what the team will produce (deliver) by the end of this meeting;
- Actions to take or topics to discuss (e.g. report student scores on the math assessment, items to review or the unit assessment, summaries of professional readings, etc.); and
- Time assigned to each action or topic.

TEAM REPORTING

By interacting across teams about what other teams are doing, team members learn more about how to be an effective team and how to tap resources from their peers on other teams.

Team logs

Teams complete brief logs or summary reports at the end of each meeting as a record of their meeting. These records become public information and help other teams and the school administrator know what progress each team is making, what challenges it is facing, and what resources or support members want. Team reports are intended to be brief yet informative. They are best completed in the last few minutes of the team's meeting by the entire team rather than by a single member.

The essential information included in a team meeting report includes:

- Members present;
- Date and time of meeting;
- Topics addressed and their link to professional and student learning goals;
- Summary comments; and
- Resources or support requested.

Sharing

Teams develop when members are willing to share their successes with other teams, model their processes, and have cross-team meetings to discuss how to strengthen the work of individual teams. An advisory team that supported the development of this resource guide suggests:

TEAMS IN A FISHBOWL

Teams are always curious about how other teams operate. One way to showcase a team's work, offer a model for others, or get support to address a challenge within a team is to ask the team to meet in a fishbowl at a faculty meeting or in another appropriate venue.

In the fishbowl, the demonstration team sits in the center of the larger group. Observers place their chairs around the outside of the circle to observe. The observers might be given specific guidelines for their role. For example, they are to watch only and may not participate in the team's work or speak to any team member during the demonstration. They may be given a process observation guide to make notes about the team's work.

Before they begin the meeting, team members might give observers a brief overview of the meeting's goals, what the team did at its last meeting, and whether feedback is desired. Then demonstration team members conduct their regular meeting, trying to forget they are being observed. Observers take notes as the meeting proceeds.

At the end of the fishbowl, a moderator facilitates as the observers question team members about their experience in the team, and the observers share their observations. If the demonstration team requests it, the observers may share some recommendations. After debriefing, the demonstration team and the observers consider these reflection questions:

- What did we learn today about effective collaborative learning teams?
- What ideas will you take away to help you strengthen your learning team?
- What challenges did you observe in the team that are similar to your team's challenges? What did you observe about how the demonstration team handled those challenges?

The meeting ends with a round of applause and a thank-you for the demonstration team.

TEAM INTERVISITATION

Inviting guests to observe team meetings is another way to help teachers from one team see what is occurring in another team. Guests may ask to visit, be invited or encouraged to visit, and will await permission from the team before visiting. When visitors observe other teams, they develop a frame of reference for their individual team's work.

Visitors will want to know the team's expectations for the visitor, and team members should determine in advance some conditions for the visit. For example, may the visitor ask questions? Offer ideas? Share resources? Critique the team's work? Offer feedback at the end of the meeting? What type of feedback? A team might ask to have the visitor comment on how the team's work links to curriculum, about the focus on specific students, proper use of a protocol, etc. A visitor should not be shy about providing feedback, particularly if the team requests it in advance.

A variation on the fishbowl and visitor strategies is

REFLECTIONS

1. What have you learned from your colleagues on other teams that has helped you or your team?

2. How would you assess your school's current cross-team interaction? To what degree do teams have a chance to learn what other teams are doing? How might other teams' work help you and your team?

3. How are current planning and reporting tools used in your school to support teams' work? To what degree are they helpful? How might you revise these tools to make them more helpful?

4. What goals might you set for cross-team collaboration for next year? What do you hope to gain? How will you know if you are successful?

5. Who is responsible for organizing cross-team collaboration and cross-team learning in your school? What strategies might you recommend to this person for increasing the amount of cross-team collaboration?

to pair two teams to observe each other, followed by partner conversations with one partner from each team discussing the similarities and differences in the ways their teams work and the work their teams accomplish.

TEAM WALK-THROUGHS

Another way for team members to learn how other teams operate is to form a small group of three to five people from various teams to conduct walk-throughs. Using the walk-through guide (**Tool 7.3** on the CD) or another they choose or construct, the group makes short visits to several teams, taking notes about what they observe.

The walk-through team meets to share observations, discuss what they saw, and prepare a brief presentation for the teams they visited about their observations. These debriefing sessions might last 15 minutes to 30 minutes, and the presentations to teams visited about 15 minutes to 20 minutes.

VIDEOTAPED PRESENTATIONS

Some schools ask teams to electronically record a team meeting and share a portion or an edited version

of the team meeting with the whole faculty. These recordings are intended to showcase the team's work, as well as how the team functions. Throughout a school year, every team might be expected to make one electronically recorded presentation of a team meeting to the entire faculty.

The recordings allow teams to identify their strengths, highlight areas they are working on, share strategies they are using to accomplish their work, offer suggestions to colleagues about how to address specific topics related to accomplishing team goals or student learning goals, or celebrate their success. Teams are more comfortable with the process of sharing their work through an electronic recording if they choose the meeting and the specific aspects of their team they want to showcase in their presentation.

FACILITATOR MEETINGS

In some schools, team facilitators meet to exchange ideas, share agendas, discuss designs for professional learning, and solve problems. Facilitators may meet with or without the school principal or other administrators. The purpose of these meetings is to support fa-

TOOL INDEX

TOOL	TITLE	USE
13.1	Sample team plan	Tool 13.1 is an example of a team's plan to organize its work and communicate the work beyond the team.
13.2	Team planning template	Tool 13.2 is a blank template for teams to use to plan.
13.3	Alternative team planning template	Tool 13.3 is an alternative team plan. Teams may use Tool 13.2 or Tool 13.3, or may create their own team planning template using the critical elements in the model tools.
13.4	Team agenda template	Tool 13.4 is a sample template for an agenda for a team plan.
13.5	Team summary report template	Tool 13.5 is a template for constructing a summary of team meetings.

cilitators in their role of managing team learning. Sometimes these meetings include learning a new protocol or design for learning. The facilitators might occasionally share issues that arise in the teams and work to solve those while maintaining confidentiality about individual team member identity. They might meet for progress updates.

When facilitators meet regularly, especially when meetings include principals, the principal stays informed about individual teams' work and can provide feedback and input on team goals and plans. Principals also then are able to assess the support teams need to accomplish their goals and to work with facilitators to access those resources. The biggest benefit of regular facilitator meetings is that facilitators learn what other teams are doing and take that information back to their own teams, using the expertise others have developed to advance their teams' work.

TEAMS TOGETHER TRANSFORM SCHOOLS

Members of collaborative professional learning teams can quickly become insular and lose touch with schoolwide goals. They lose the seamlessness among a faculty that ensures the curriculum is implemented and reinforced, builds on individual student learning needs, and provides continuous assessment for and of learning. Without frequent interaction with the whole faculty and other teams, teams lose perspective and their sense of collective responsibility. Yet, because time is a nonrenewable resource, school leaders and team members often hesitate to take time for interteam sharing, even if that sharing is simply posting team plans, logs, and products.

Each team is, however, integrally connected to every other team in the school. It is vital that they learn to share and to connect with each other beyond the team to maintain focus, provide support and assistance, and accomplish their goals.

REFERENCE

Hargreaves, A. & Fullan, M. (1998). *What's worth fighting for out there?* New York: Teachers College Press.

Chapter 14

EVALUATING
collaborative professional learning

WHERE ARE WE NOW?

Collaborative professional learning teams use evidence to evaluate the impact of their work in achieving their professional learning goals.

STRONGLY AGREE	AGREE	NO OPINION	DISAGREE	STRONGLY DISAGREE

Collaborative professional learning team members use formative evaluation to assess the impact of their learning on student achievement.

STRONGLY AGREE	AGREE	NO OPINION	DISAGREE	STRONGLY DISAGREE

Collaborative professional learning team members use summative evaluation to assess the impact of their learning on student achievement.

STRONGLY AGREE	AGREE	NO OPINION	DISAGREE	STRONGLY DISAGREE

Members of collaborative professional learning teams assess their team's productivity and efficiency.

STRONGLY AGREE	AGREE	NO OPINION	DISAGREE	STRONGLY DISAGREE

Members of collaborative professional learning teams provide one another with feedback about their individual contribution to the team.

STRONGLY AGREE	AGREE	NO OPINION	DISAGREE	STRONGLY DISAGREE

To improve collaborative professional learning, teams regularly evaluate their work. For many years, staff development evaluations focused on whether participants enjoyed their learning experiences. Today's evaluations ask more sophisticated questions. Professional learning leaders want to know if professional development is creating changes in teacher practice and in student learning.

Evaluations can focus on four aspects of the work: team efficiency, team effectiveness, individual members' contributions, and members' effect on practice and student learning. Teams that periodically assess and analyze the results of assessments in each of these areas will find valuable data they can use to strengthen their work. Tools on the CD for this chapter will help teams and others refine and improve teacher practices and results.

The first step for principals, teams, school leadership teams, and even district staff who want to evaluate collaborative professional learning is to determine how rigorous they want the evaluation to be and what they want to know as a result.

Most schools begin their evaluation of collaborative professional learning teams with a less comprehensive, less sophisticated approach to evaluation. They use informal, formative assessments. Some school or district leaders, however, may want a more formal evaluation as part of the district's and school's overall evaluation of professional learning programs. External evaluations, such as those conducted by the principal, also are useful to collaborative professional learning teams. Indeed, one of the principal's responsibilities (see Chapter 7) is providing regular feedback about the teams' work and processes.

Finding out whether teams are meeting their goals doesn't require an academic research study. The tools on the CD for this chapter are designed to make evaluation meaningful, beneficial, and practical for those wanting either informal or formal evaluations of collaborative professional learning.

THEORY OF CHANGE

Evaluation designs are based on what evaluators want to know and what they are evaluating. Evaluators may choose from a range of evaluation designs to assess collaborative professional learning. **Tool 14.1** is a

Figure 14.1 PROPOSED CORE CONCEPTUAL FRAMEWORK FOR STUDYING THE EFFECTS OF PROFESSIONAL DEVELOPMENT ON TEACHERS AND STUDENTS

Core features of professional development:

- Content focus
- Active learning
- Coherence
- Duration
- Collective participation

- Increased teacher knowledge and skills
- Change in attitudes and beliefs

Change in instruction

Improved student learning

Source: Desimone, L. (2009). Improving impact studies of teachers' professional development: Toward better conceptualizations and measures. *Educational Researcher, 38*(3), 181-199.

primer on evaluation, including a sample evaluation design. For a deeper understanding of the evaluation process, consult *Assessing Impact: Evaluating Staff Development* (Killion, 2008). The book proposes using a theory of change approach to evaluating professional learning that today is gaining ground. Laura Desimone (2009) proposes a theory of change model similar to ones found in *Assessing Impact*. Desimone's theory appears in **Figure 14.1.**

FORMATIVE AND SUMMATIVE EVALUATION

Teams conduct two kinds of evaluation — formative and summative. Formative evaluations concentrate on the team's processes for efficiency, its completion of planned actions, and the outcomes of those actions. Summative evaluations focus on whether the team succeeds in meeting its goals. These goals, stated as SMART (specific, measurable, attainable, results-oriented, time-bound) goals, are focused on improving teaching quality and student learning.

Formative evaluation

A formative assessment looks at how well teams work, their actions, and the interim outcomes they produce.

Those evaluating professional learning often note an action itself as evidence rather than its results. For example, if a team read a research summary, some evaluators would document that 98% of the teachers read the research. However, the result is not how many read the summary, but what changed as a consequence. The result of reading the summary would be the extent to which team members increased their knowledge. In another example, some evaluators might count how many hours teachers met in teams, but that number does not tell whether collaborative professional learning is working to change teaching practice and student learning. Counting meeting hours does nothing to bring to light what changes occurred in daily classroom practice.

Evaluators work with team members to decide what outcomes the team wants from each planned action and to measure the results of those actions. A logic model drives this form of evaluation (Killion, 2008). A logic model has five main components (see **Figure 14.2**):

- Inputs/resources;
- Actions;
- Initial outcomes;
- Intermediate outcomes; and
- Results.

A logic model links inputs (resources) to actions

Figure 14.2 LOGIC MODEL COMPONENTS

Inputs/resources	Actions	Initial outcomes	Intermediate outcomes	Results
The school, district, community, or state resources (including people, space, time, equipment, or materials) needed to accomplish the actions.	The sequence of activities the team plans to take to accomplish its goal(s), using the resources identified.	The early results of the actions, e.g. what happens initially when the action is completed; initial outcomes often describe changes in knowledge and skills.	The secondary results of the actions, e.g. what happens after the initial outcomes occur; intermediate outcomes often describe changes in behavior or practice.	The SMART goal(s) the team sets for its professional learning.
Planned actions		Intended results		

(steps to accomplish the results) and identifies initial outcomes (first changes expected from the actions) and intermediate outcomes (subsequent changes that occur after the initial outcomes) in a logical way to explain how the actions will produce the desired result — student learning.

A sample logic model for collaborative professional learning teams is shown in **Table 14.1**. Teams that develop and use a logic model have a sound way to plan their actions and identify what they expect to see as evidence that their actions are successful and to assess their progress toward those goal(s).

By looking at the outcomes of their actions rather than whether the action was completed, teams have a better measure of the impact of their actions. In addition, they have the capacity to look at the interaction that occurs between their work and student learning.

Figure 14.3 shows a theory of change that describes how teacher learning affects teaching quality and student learning. How teachers and students understand the learning and their motivation become factors in the success of any professional learning.

Not all schools will develop a logic model for their evaluation. However, if they decide to do so, they will have a clearer understanding of the outcomes they seek to produce and the kind of evidence needed to measure if those outcomes have been achieved. Tools such as the surveys and Innovation Configurations are instruments for measuring change.

A team can become more productive by periodically collecting members' perceptions of the team's functioning and discussing the data. **Tools 14.2** and **14.3** are two surveys for assessing teams. Members might examine their efficiency by focusing on whether they have in place the meeting structures typical of successful teams. Individual members can evaluate their own involvement on the team. Team members can learn how the team is doing overall by aggregating individuals' ratings into a single mean score, identifying the range (highest score and lowest score), and determining the score that occurs most frequently for each item. Team members then can use the guidelines in **Tool 14.4** to discuss survey results. The protocol is general enough to be used for both surveys or for each independently.

Teams also can draw from these surveys to create their own, starting with simple surveys if members have not assessed team effectiveness before or are new to the concept of collaborative professional learning teams. **Tool 14.2** is more appropriate for teams in beginning

Table 14.1 SAMPLE LOGIC MODEL FOR COLLABORATIVE PROFESSIONAL LEARNING TEAMS

Inputs/resources	Actions	Initial outcomes	Intermediate outcomes	Results
Teaching resources for unit development. Team meeting time to score baseline writing assessments, develop units and common assessments, analyze student results, form and re-evaluate flexible groupings, etc.	Analyze data from fall writing sample.	Teachers identify students' baseline writing level.	Teachers group students in flexible groupings for instruction in conventions, ideas, and organization.	20% increase in student scores on the state writing sample in two years.
Support from district language arts specialist to assist with design of units.	Design three common instructional units for ideas and organization to use between October and February.	Teachers use units in their classrooms.	Students practice applying ideas and organization in writing assignments in all content areas.	
Support from the district language arts specialist to assist with the development of common writing assessments.	Develop and administer two common benchmark assessments of writing, one in November and one in February.	Teachers administer and score common assessments.	Teachers analyze data from the assessments to determine which students require reteaching and additional support.	
Cooperation of science and social studies teachers to embed the use of ideas, organization, and conventions in their writing scoring tools.	Develop daily practice activities for language conventions.	Students complete daily activity to practice language conventions.	Students demonstrate increased accuracy in use of language conventions in both oral and written language.	
Suppport from teachers to provide feedback and additional instruction to students on ideas, organization, and conventions.	Provide students ongoing feedback, reteaching, and additional support, as needed, on ideas, organization, and conventions.	Students' accurate use of ideas, organization, and conventions increases in their classroom work.	Students' accurate use of ideas, organization, and conventions increases on common benchmark assessments.	

Figure 14.3 BLACK BOXES OF TEACHER AND STUDENT LEARNING

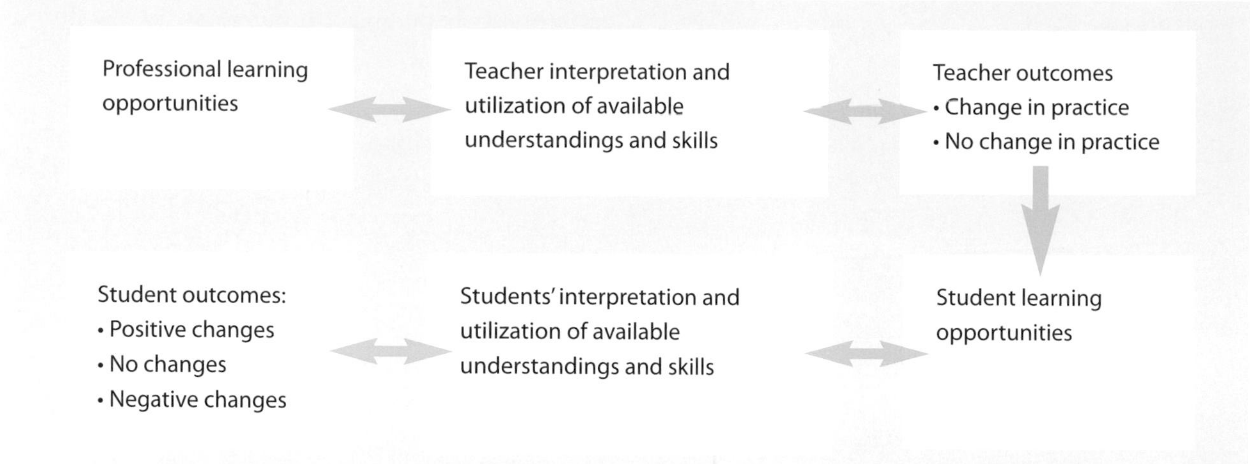

Source: **Timperley, H. & Alton-Lee, A. (2008).** Reframing teacher professional learning: An alternative policy approach to strengthening valued outcomes for diverse learners. *Review of Reseach in Education, 32*(1), 328-369.

stages, while **Tool 14.3** is for teams that are more advanced in working collaboratively and are ready to move to the next level and become high-performing teams.

Team members might use the Learning School Innovation Configuration Map, **Tool 14.5**, to evaluate the team's effectiveness. Unlike the surveys, which assess perceptions, the Innovation Configuration describes essential behaviors of the school leadership team, teacher leaders (coaches), teams, and individual teachers. Teams might use their results to gauge progress over time if they set a baseline and compare subsequent measures. To use the Innovation Configuration:

Ask team members to individually identify where they think their team is on the continuum.

Compile the results, using the level number from each person's response. If team members have developed trust or decide voluntarily to share their results publicly, have each member respond, and compile the results on a wall chart for all to see. Use the protocol in **Tool 14.4** to discuss the results.

NSDC's Standards Assessment Inventory (www.nsdc.org/standards/sai.cfm) is another reliable way to assess collaborative, standards-based professional learning within a school.

Some teachers are comfortable with their current practices and hesitate to change. Yet if teachers engage in professional learning and apply that learning to their classroom practices, student achievement will change. If teachers want to know whether professional development had an impact on teaching quality that then affected student academic success, they need some form of formative evaluation.

Summative evaluation

A summative evaluation helps teams determine whether members achieved their goal(s). Summative evaluations occur at the end of a planned action. Teams define the success of their learning by whether students perform at expected levels. Sometimes teams will not be able to determine if they met their goal until they receive state assessment results. Because there is substantial lag time between the administration of some state assessments and the results, collaborative professional learning teams may want to consider using common assessments as one measure of student success. While common assessments may lack the rigor of state assess-

REFLECTIONS

1. Given our school's involvement in collaborative professional learning, what kind of evaluation best suits our needs? What is the purpose of our evaluation? How are we using the results now?

2. How can formative evaluation assist teams in improving their work? How does summative evaluation contribute to the success of teams' work?

3. How rigorous does our evaluation of collaborative professional learning need to be?

4. What do we hope to learn about our work from our evaluation?

5. What do we do with our evaluation findings? How can we share them with other teams to strengthen teacher collaboration in the school?

ments, they offer team members some information about their success in a more timely manner.

In addition to determining if teams collectively attained their goals, a school's leadership or professional development team may want to determine if the school culture has improved since teams are working collaboratively to learn as professionals.

Using the school culture survey in **Tool 3.2** as a pre- and post-test, staff members might complete the survey as a baseline in the fall and again near the end of the school year. By looking at the differences, learning teams have influenced the school's culture. Staff members will not be able to conclude that collaborative professional learning has caused the changes in culture, although it will be safe to conclude that collaborative professional learning has contributed to the change. Such a conclusion can be strengthened if teams have demonstrated increased efficiency and effectiveness as a team and if they have used a logic model to determine if their intended outcomes have been achieved.

As a summative measure of team development and success, staff members may want to use **Tool 14.7** to assess how the team is functioning. At the end of each school year or possibly at the midpoint in a school year, a collaborative professional learning team will benefit from taking time to have a discussion guided by the summative reflection protocol in **Tool 14.8.**

To assess the use of collaborative teams, **Tools 14.9** and **14.10** are included. These tools can be used as a pre- and post-test measure of the team's effectiveness.

The surveys in this chapter are examples. Making adjustments in the survey instruments or using part of the samples included is acceptable. What is unacceptable is avoiding evaluation of how collaborative professional learning is influencing teacher collaboration, the school culture, and student learning.

REFERENCES

Desimone, L. (2009). Improving impact studies of teachers' professional development: Toward better conceptualizations and measures. *Educational Researcher, 38*(3), 181-199.

Killion, J. (2008). *Assessing impact: Evaluating staff development* (2nd ed.). Thousand Oaks, CA: Corwin Press & NSDC.

Timperley, H. & Alton-Lee, A. (2008). Reframing teacher professional learning: An alternative policy approach to strengthening valued outcomes for diverse learners. *Review of Research in Education, 32*(1), 328-369.

Tool 14.5

Learning School Innovation Configuration Map

T he Learning School Innovation Configuration Map is a planning and assessment tool for use by school leadership teams and collaborative professional learning teams to ensure full implementation of NSDC's definition of professional development and the system structures needed to support collaborative professional learning. Learning schools work to achieve Level 1 in each component area over time.

An Innovation Configuration (IC) map describes

in behavioral terms what key stakeholders do in a learning school. It also describes variations of the ideal or best practices in a learning school along a continuum that describes the progression schools make over time along the road to become a learning school. As a planning tool, the IC map guides a school's leadership team and teams of teachers in the identification of specific actions to progress toward the desired outcome. As an assessment tool, the IC map serves as a guide to determine the current state of the school's implementation of the definition. The planning and assessment functions of the IC map work hand-in-hand to guide school leadership teams and collaborative professional learning teams to establish the context and processes of effective learning schools.

Author's note: With special appreciation to Shirley Hord, NSDC's scholar laureate, and Stephanie Hirsh, NSDC's executive director, for their counsel, review, and guidance in the development of these IC maps.

Tool 14.5 LEARNING SCHOOL INNOVATION CONFIGURATION MAP, continued

COMPREHENSIVE, SUSTAINED, INTENSIVE PROFESSIONAL LEARNING

Outcome 1: In a learning school, the school leadership team, teacher leaders (coaches), teams of teachers, and individual teachers engage in effective professional learning.

EFFECTIVENESS

1.1: The school leadership team, teacher leaders (coaches), teams of teachers, and individual teachers engage in comprehensive, sustained, and intensive professional learning to improve teachers' and principals' effectiveness in raising student achievement.

Level 1	Level 2	Level 3	Level 4	Level 5	Level 6
Engage in intentional, comprehensive, sustained, and intensive professional learning focused on raising student achievement by improving teaching quality and leadership.	Engage in intentional, comprehensive, sustained, and intensive professional learning focused on raising student achievement by improving teaching quality.	Engage in intentional, comprehensive, sustained, and intensive professional learning focused on multiple topics.	Engage in short-term, intentional, professional learning focused on raising student achievement by improving teaching quality and leadership.	Engage in short-term, intentional, professional learning focused on raising student achievement by improving teaching quality.	Engage in occasional, intentional, professional learning focused on a variety of topics.

COLLECTIVE RESPONSIBILITY

1.2: The school leadership team, teacher leaders (coaches), teams of teachers, and individual teachers share collective responsibility for student learning.

Level 1	Level 2	Level 3	Level 4	Level 5	Level 6
Work and learn together sharing collective responsibility so that each individual and team contributes to the success of ALL students within the school.	Work and learn together sharing collective responsibility so that each team contributes to the success of its students.	Work and learn together so that each individual team member can improve the success of his or her students.	Acknowledge that they have limited responsibility for student learning.	Hold nonschool factors responsible for student performance.	Disregard factors that influence student academic success.

Tool 14.5 LEARNING SCHOOL INNOVATION CONFIGURATION MAP, continued

TEAM CONFIGURATION

1.3: The school leadership team, teacher leaders (coaches), teams of teachers, and individual teachers meet in a variety of team configurations over time addressing specific goals for teacher and student learning.

Level 1	Level 2	Level 3	Level 4	Level 5	Level 6
Meet in a variety of team configurations over time, addressing specific goals for teacher and student learning, including vertical and whole-school problem or topic-focused school improvement teams and grade-level, department, or course teams with members who share common curriculum and/or students.	Meet in a variety of team configurations over time, addressing specific goals for teacher and student learning, including grade-level, department, or course teams with members who share common curriculum or students, or project teams for school improvement.	Meet in a variety of team configurations over time, addressing specific goals for teacher and student learning, including grade-level, department, or course teams.	Meet over time in a single team, addressing specific goals for teacher and student learning, school improvement, and student results.	Work independently addressing specific goals for teacher and student learning.	Work independently without focus on specific goals for teacher and student learning.

FREQUENCY

1.4: The school leadership team, teacher leaders (coaches), teams of teachers, and individual teachers make time for professional learning several times per week.

Level 1	Level 2	Level 3	Level 4	Level 5	Level 6
Meet several times per week within the school day for teacher collaborative team meetings and periodic whole-school collaboration.	Meet each week within the school day for teacher collaborative team meetings and periodic whole-school collaboration.	Meet biweekly within the school day for teacher collaborative team meetings and periodic whole-school collaboration.	Meet each month within the school day for teacher collaborative team meetings and periodic whole-school collaboration.	Meet several days per school year within the school day for teacher collaborative team meetings and whole-school collaboration.	Meet outside the school day for teacher collaborative meetings and whole-school collaboration.

Tool 14.5 LEARNING SCHOOL INNOVATION CONFIGURATION MAP, continued

CONTINUOUS CYCLE OF IMPROVEMENT

Outcome 2: Learning teams use a cycle of continuous improvement to refine teaching quality and improve student learning.

DATA ANALYSIS

2.1: Learning teams engage in ongoing data analysis of teacher and student performance to determine school, educator, and student learning goals.

Level 1	Level 2	Level 3	Level 4	Level 5	Level 6
Analyze multiple types of data (achievement, process, demographic, and perception) at the school, team, and classroom levels throughout the school year to identify student strengths and weaknesses to set annual goals for student growth and teacher learning; analyze multiple types of data at the school, team, and classroom levels several times throughout the school year to measure progress toward annual goals for student and teacher learning, to set benchmark goals for teacher and student learning, and to make ongoing adjustments in both goals and strategies for attaining the goals.	Analyze student achievement and demographic data at the school, team, and classroom levels throughout the school year to identify student strengths and weaknesses to set annual goals for student growth and teacher learning; analyze student achievement and demographic data at the school, team, and classroom levels several times throughout the school year to measure progress toward annual goals for student and teacher learning, to set benchmark goals for teacher and student learning, and to make ongoing adjustments in both goals and strategies for attaining the goals.	Analyze student achievement data at the school, team, and classroom levels throughout the school year to identify student strengths and weaknesses to set annual goals for student growth and teacher learning; analyze student achievement data at the school, team, and classroom levels several times throughout the school year to measure progress toward annual goals for student and teacher learning, to set benchmark goals for teacher and student learning, and to make ongoing adjustments in both goals and strategies for attaining the goals.	Analyze student achievement data at the school level throughout the school year to identify student strengths and weaknesses to set annual goals for student growth and teacher learning; analyze student achievement data at the school, team, and classroom levels several times throughout the school year to measure progress toward annual goals for student and teacher learning, and to set benchmark goals for teacher and student learning.	Analyze student achievement data at the school level throughout the school year to identify student strengths and weaknesses to set annual goals for student growth and teacher learning; analyze student achievement data at the school, team, and classroom levels several times throughout the school year to measure progress toward annual goals for student and teacher learning.	Analyze student achievement data at the school level throughout the school year to identify student strengths and weaknesses to set annual goals for student growth.

National Staff Development Council · www.nsdc.org

Tool 14.5 LEARNING SCHOOL INNOVATION CONFIGURATION MAP, continued

STUDENT LEARNING GOALS

2.2: Learning teams set goals for student learning.

Level 1	Level 2	Level 3	Level 4	Level 5	Level 6
Write annual and benchmark SMART (specific, measurable, attainable, results-oriented, time-bound) goals for student achievement based on school, team, and classroom data to guide their planning and improvement efforts and revise those goals throughout the school year.	Write annual and benchmark SMART (specific, measurable, attainable, results-oriented, time-bound) goals for student achievement based on school, team, and classroom data to guide their planning and improvement efforts and revise those goals throughout the school year.	Write annual SMART (specific, measurable, attainable, results-oriented, time-bound) goals for student achievement based on school, team, and classroom data to guide their planning and improvement efforts.	Receive annual SMART (specific, measurable, attainable, results-oriented, time-bound) goals for student achievement based on schoolwide data to guide their planning and improvement efforts.	Receive annual SMART (specific, measurable, attainable, results-oriented, time-bound) goals for student achievement based on districtwide data to guide their planning and improvement efforts.	Receive annual goals for student achievement based on districtwide data to guide their planning and improvement efforts.

EDUCATOR LEARNING GOALS

2.3: Learning teams write goals for educator learning aligned with student learning goals to guide professional learning.

Level 1	Level 2	Level 3	Level 4	Level 5	Level 6
Write annual and benchmark professional learning goals for the school and teams aligned with student learning goals and revise those goals throughout the school year.	Write annual and benchmark professional learning goals for the school and teams aligned with student learning goals.	Write annual professional learning goals for the school aligned with student learning goals.	Use district professional learning goals to guide adult learning within the school and team.	Use district professional learning goals to guide adult learning within the school.	Use topics rather than goals to guide professional learning within the school.

Tool 14.5 LEARNING SCHOOL INNOVATION CONFIGURATION MAP, continued

MULTIPLE DESIGNS

2.4: Learning teams select and implement multiple designs for professional learning aligned with NSDC's Standards for Staff Development to develop knowledge, attitudes, skills, aspirations, and behaviors necessary to support advanced levels of student learning.

Level 1	Level 2	Level 3	Level 4	Level 5	Level 6
Select, with broad-based input from teacher leaders and teachers, and implement multiple selected designs for team and whole-school professional learning that align with educator and student learning goals and support and encourage collaborative inquiry, problem solving, and learning among educators.	Select, with broad-based input from teacher leaders and teachers, and implement two selected designs for team and whole-school professional learning that align with educator and student learning goals and support and encourage collaborative inquiry, problem solving, and learning among educators.	Select, with broad-based input from teacher leaders and teachers, and implement a single design for team and whole-school professional learning that align with educator and student learning goals and support and encourage collaborative inquiry, problem solving, and learning among educators.	Implement multiple selected designs for team and whole-school professional learning aligned with student learning goals with limited input from teacher leaders and teachers.	Implement a single design for team and whole-school professional learning aligned with student learning goals with limited input from teacher leaders and teachers.	Implement designs for team- and whole-school professional learning selected by someone outside the school without input from teacher leaders and teachers.

Tool 14.5 LEARNING SCHOOL INNOVATION CONFIGURATION MAP, continued

INTERVENTIONS FOR STUDENT LEARNING

2.5: Learning teams select or develop research-based, coherent, classroom-centered interventions for student learning.

Level 1	Level 2	Level 3	Level 4	Level 5	Level 6
Select and/or develop research-based, coherent, classroom-centered interventions for student learning that align with team and student learning goals, focus on the school's instructional framework for teaching quality, and emphasize changes in teacher practice to promote student learning.	Select and/or develop research-based, coherent, classroom-centered interventions for student learning that align with team and student learning goals and focus on the school's instructional framework for teaching quality.	Select and/or develop research-based, coherent, classroom-centered interventions for student learning that align with team and student learning goals.	Select and/or develop classroom-centered interventions for student learning that align with team and student learning goals.	Select and/or develop school-centered interventions for student learning that align with team and student learning goals.	Select and/or develop nonclassroom- and nonschool-centered interventions for student learning.

Tool 14.5 LEARNING SCHOOL INNOVATION CONFIGURATION MAP, continued

JOB-EMBEDDED SUPPORT

2.6: The school leadership team, teacher leaders (coaches), and team members provide ongoing support at the classroom level to implement educator learning to increase student achievement.

Level 1	Level 2	Level 3	Level 4	Level 5	Level 6
Provide continuous job-embedded coaching and other forms of classroom-based support (e.g. peer observation, instructional, walk-throughs, demonstration lessons, etc.) to transfer educator learning to classroom and schoolwide practice to increase student achievement.	Provide periodic job-embedded coaching and other forms of classroom-based support (e.g. peer observation, instructional, walk-throughs, demonstration lessons, etc.) to transfer educator learning to classroom and schoolwide practice to increase student achievement.	Provide occasional job-embedded coaching and other forms of classroom-based support (e.g. peer observation, instructional, walk-throughs, demonstration lessons, etc.) to transfer educator learning to classroom and schoolwide practice to increase student achievement.	Provide one opportunity for job-embedded coaching and other forms of classroom-based support (e.g. peer observation, instructional, walk-throughs, demonstration lessons, etc.) to transfer educator learning to classroom and schoolwide practice to increase student achievement.	Provide no job-embedded coaching or other forms of classroom-based support (e.g. peer observation, instructional, walk-throughs, demonstration lessons, etc.) to transfer educator learning to classroom and schoolwide practice to increase student achievement.	

ONGOING EVALUATION

2.7: Learning teams evaluate the effectiveness of professional learning.

Level 1	Level 2	Level 3	Level 4	Level 5	Level 6
Assess regularly (multiple times per year) the effectiveness of professional learning in achieving identified educator and student learning goals, improving teaching, and assisting all students in meeting academic standards.	Assess semiannually the effectiveness of professional learning in achieving identified educator and student learning goals, improving teaching, and assisting all students in meeting academic standards.	Assess annually the effectiveness of professional learning in achieving identified educator and student learning goals, improving teaching, and assisting all students in meeting academic standards.	Assess over multiple years the effectiveness of professional learning in achieving identified educator and student learning goals, improving teaching, and assisting all students in meeting academic standards.	Conduct no assessment of the effectiveness of professional learning in achieving identified educator and student learning goals, improving teaching, and assisting all students in meeting academic standards.	

Tool 14.5 LEARNING SCHOOL INNOVATION CONFIGURATION MAP, continued

EXPANDED OPPORTUNITIES FOR PROFESSIONAL LEARNING

Outcome 3: In a learning school, the school leadership team, teacher leaders (coaches), and teacher teams access external assistance to provide teams with expanded opportunities for professional learning, additional resources, and expert guidance to support team learning and goal attainment.

EXTERNAL ASSISTANCE

3.1: Learning teams, school leadership teams, and teacher leaders (coaches) access external assistance to extend educator and student learning goals.

Level 1	Level 2	Level 3	Level 4	Level 5	Level 6
Access external assistance providers within and outside the school system to support the implementation of collaborative professional learning and help the team reach its professional learning goals and student learning goals by expanding opportunities within the school for professional learning, sharing resources, offering guidance, and assessing effectiveness and impact.	Access external assistance providers within and outside the school system to support the implementation of collaborative professional learning and help the team reach its professional learning goals and student learning goals by expanding opportunities outside the school for professional learning, sharing resources, offering guidance, and assessing effectiveness and impact.	Access external assistance providers within and outside the school system to support the implementation of collaborative professional learning and help the team reach its professional learning goals and student learning goals by expanding opportunities outside the school for professional learning.	Access external assistance providers within and outside the school system to support the implementation of collaborative professional learning and help the team reach its student learning goals.	Access external assistance providers within and outside the school system to support the implementation of collaborative professional learning and assist the team in reaching its professional learning goals.	Access no external assistance to support the implementation of collaborative professional learning, team learning goals, individual learning goals, or student learning goals.

Tool 14.5 LEARNING SCHOOL INNOVATION CONFIGURATION MAP, continued

LEARNING OUTSIDE THE SCHOOL

3.2: The school leadership team, teacher leaders (coaches), teams of teachers, and individual teachers participate in learning outside the school.

Level 1	Level 2	Level 3	Level 4	Level 5	Level 6
Participate in professional learning offered by the central office or organizations outside the school district when there is clear evidence that the learning aligns with a team or school learning goal and there is a commitment to apply the learning schoolwide, in teams, or in classrooms as appropriate, and to assess the impact of such actions.	Participate in professional learning offered by the central office or organizations outside the school district when there is clear evidence that the learning aligns with a team or school learning goal and there is a commitment to apply the learning schoolwide, in teams, or classroom as appropriate.	Participate in professional learning offered by the central office or organizations outside the school district when there is clear evidence that the learning aligns with a team or school learning goal.	May participate in learning events offered by the central office and/or organizations outside the school district.	May participate in learning events offered by the central office.	Participate in no learning events outside the school.

Tool 14.5 LEARNING SCHOOL INNOVATION CONFIGURATION MAP, continued

EVALUATION OF COLLABORATIVE PROFESSIONAL LEARNING

Outcome 4: In learning schools, the school leadership team, teacher leaders (coaches), and teacher teams evaluate the collaborative professional learning to make improvements.

ONGOING EVALUATION

4.1: The school leadership team, teacher leaders (coaches), teams of teachers, and individual teachers evaluate collaborative professional learning on an ongoing basis.

Level 1	Level 2	Level 3	Level 4	Level 5	Level 6
Engage in ongoing evaluation using multiple sources of data to assess team results, operations, and individual members' contribution to teams and to adjust their efforts.	Engage in ongoing evaluation using a single source of data to assess team results, operations and individual members' contribution to teams and to adjust their efforts.	Engage in ongoing evaluation using multiple sources of data to assess team results and operations and to adjust their efforts.	Engage in ongoing evaluation using multiple sources of data to assess team results and operations.	Engage in intermittent evaluation to assess team results, operations, and individual members' contribution to teams.	Engage in intermittent evaluation to assess team results and operations.

Tool 14.5 LEARNING SCHOOL INNOVATION CONFIGURATION MAP, continued

SCHOOL SUPPORT FOR COLLABORATIVE PROFESSIONAL LEARNING

Outcome 5: In learning schools, principals, teacher leaders (coaches), and teachers support staff collaboration.

PRINCIPAL SUPPORT

5.1: Principals set expectations for, support, monitor, and evaluate collaborative professional learning.

Level 1	Level 2	Level 3	Level 4	Level 5	Level 6
Set expectations for all staff to engage in collaborative professional learning; provide support for teams; ensure that teams have professional learning on effective team functioning; monitor team plans, goals, and progress; meet periodically with teams to assess their operation; meet regularly with team leaders to discuss teams' work and progress; review team logs; and hold regular cross-team meetings to share what teams are learning for the benefit of the whole faculty.	Set expectations for all staff to engage in collaborative professional learning; ensure that teams have professional learning on effective team functioning; monitor team plans, goals, and progress; monitor team plans, goals, and progress by participating in team meetings and meeting with team leaders to discuss team processes and outcomes.	Set expectations for all staff to engage in collaborative professional learning; provide support for teams; ensure that teams have professional learning on effective team functioning; monitor team plans, goals, and progress by meeting periodically with teams to assess their operation and by reviewing team logs.	Set expectations for all staff to engage in collaborative professional learning; ensure that teams have professional learning on effective team functioning; monitor team plans, goals, and progress by reviewing team logs.	Set expectations for all staff to engage in collaborative professional learning; monitor team plans, goals, and progress by reviewing team logs.	Set expectations for all staff to engage in collaborative professional learning.

Tool 14.5 LEARNING SCHOOL INNOVATION CONFIGURATION MAP, continued

TEACHER LEADER SUPPORT

5.2: In learning schools, teacher leaders (coaches) support collaborative professional learning.

Level 1	Level 2	Level 3	Level 4	Level 5	Level 6
Facilitate team data analysis, planning, learning, work, and evaluation to model and teach the team how to learn and work independently over time; gradually release team leadership to teams over time; provide learning opportunities for team members and faculty on the collaborative professional learning process; provide learning opportunities for team leaders to learn effective facilitation and learning designs; coach team leaders to become skillful in leading collaborative professional learning; facilitate meetings of team leaders to problem solve and develop new strategies to support team learning and work.	Facilitate team data analysis, planning, learning, work, and evaluation to model and teach the team how to learn and work independently over time; provide learning opportunities for team members and faculty on the collaborative professional learning process; provide learning opportunities for team leaders to learn effective facilitation and learning designs; coach team leaders to become skillful in leading collaborative professional learning; facilitate meetings of team leaders to problem solve and develop new strategies to support team learning and work.	Facilitate team data analysis, planning, learning, work, and evaluation to model and teach the team how to learn and work independently over time; provide learning opportunities for team members and faculty on the collaborative professional learning process; provide learning opportunities for team leaders to learn effective facilitation and learning designs; facilitate meetings of team leaders to problem solve and develop new strategies to support team learning and work.	Facilitate team data analysis, planning, learning, work, and evaluation to model and teach the team how to learn and work independently over time; provide learning opportunities for team members and faculty on the collaborative professional learning process; provide learning opportunities for team leaders to learn effective facilitation and learning designs.	Provide learning opportunities for team members and faculty on the collaborative professional learning process; provide learning opportunities for team leaders to learn effective facilitation and learning designs.	Provide learning opportunities for team members and faculty on the collaborative professional learning process.

Tool 14.5 LEARNING SCHOOL INNOVATION CONFIGURATION MAP, continued

TEACHER SUPPORT

5.3: In learning schools, teachers actively participate in multiple learning teams.

Level 1	Level 2	Level 3	Level 4	Level 5	Level 6
Participate in multiple teams, including a grade-level, department, or course-focused learning team, to accomplish educator and student learning goals, whole-school learning team focused on student and educator schoolwide learning goals, or grade-level, content-area, and course teams focused on vertical alignment of curriculum, assessment, and instruction; meet the expectations for full participation as a team member; contribute to the team's learning and work; reflect as a team on individual and team progress toward professional learning goals and student learning goals.	Participate in multiple teams, including a grade-level, department, or course-focused learning team, to accomplish educator and student learning goals, whole-school learning team focused on student and educator schoolwide learning goals or cross grade-level, content-area, and course teams focused on vertical alignment of curriculum, assessment, and instruction; contribute to the team's learning and work; reflect as a team on individual and team progress toward professional learning goals and student learning goals.	Participate in multiple teams, including a grade-level, department, or course-focused learning team, to accomplish educator and student learning goals, whole-school learning team focused on student and educator schoolwide learning goals, or cross grade-level, content-area, and course teams focused on vertical alignment of curriculum, assessment, and instruction.	Participate in a single team, including a grade-level, department, or course-focused learning team, to accomplish educator and student learning goals, whole-school learning team focused on student and educator schoolwide learning goals, or content-area and course teams focused on vertical alignment of curriculum, assessment, and instruction; meet the expectations for full participation as a team member; contribute to the team's learning and work; reflect as a team on individual and team progress toward professional learning goals and student learning goals.	Participate in a single team, including a grade-level, department, or course-focused learning team, to accomplish educator and student learning goals, whole-school learning team focused on student and educator schoolwide learning goals, or content-area and course teams focused on vertical alignment of curriculum, assessment, and instruction; contribute to the team's learning and work; reflect as a team on individual and team progress toward professional learning goals and student learning goals.	Participate in a single team, including a grade-level, department, or course-focused learning team, to accomplish educator and student learning goals.

Tool 14.5 LEARNING SCHOOL INNOVATION CONFIGURATION MAP, continued

CLASSROOM IMPLEMENTATION

5.4: In learning schools, teachers implement and reflect on their learning in their classrooms.

Level 1	Level 2	Level 3	Level 4	Level 5	Level 6
Implement learning from collaborative professional learning teams in the classroom; gather data from the classroom to share with the team to assess effectiveness of the intervention; report to team members the effect of interventions on student learning; adapt instruction and classroom curriculum to align with student learning needs and goals; reflect on individual progress toward professional learning goals and student learning goals.	Implement learning from collaborative professional learning teams in the classroom; gather data from the classroom to share with the team to assess effectiveness of the intervention; report to team members the effect of interventions on student learning; adapt instruction and classroom curriculum to align with student learning needs and goals; reflect on individual progress toward professional learning goals and student learning goals.	Implement learning from collaborative professional learning teams in the classroom; adapt instruction and classroom curriculum to align with student learning needs and goals; reflect on individual progress toward professional learning.	Implement learning from collaborative professional learning teams in the classroom; adapt instruction and classroom curriculum to align with student learning needs and goals.	Implement learning from collaborative professional learning teams in the classroom.	

Tool 14.5 LEARNING SCHOOL INNOVATION CONFIGURATION MAP, continued

DISTRICT SUPPORT FOR COLLABORATIVE PROFESSIONAL LEARNING

Outcome 6: Learning schools receive support from district leaders who support collaborative professional learning through policy, resources, expectations, professional learning, and ongoing support.

DISTRICT LEADER SUPPORT

6.1: District leaders support learning schools.

Level 1	Level 2	Level 3	Level 4	Level 5	Level 6
Advocate for school board policies, guidance documents, and district structures to support collaborative professional learning and embed collaborative learning teams in both principal and teacher performance standards; communicate the importance of collaborative professional learning to the community; allocate resources to support collaborative professional learning; engage district and school leaders in collaborative professional learning teams; provide professional learning and ongoing support for principals and teacher leaders (coaches) on leading, facilitating, supporting, and monitoring collaborative professional learning teams; develop and support teacher leaders (coaches) to facilitate learning teams; coordinate ongoing cross-school collaboration to share successes and address challenges.	Allocate resources to support collaborative professional learning; engage district and school leaders in collaborative professional learning teams; provide professional learning and ongoing support for principals and teacher leaders (coaches) on leading, facilitating, supporting, and monitoring collaborative professional learning teams; develop and support teacher leaders (coaches) to facilitate learning teams; coordinate ongoing cross-school collaboration to share successes and address challenges.	Allocate resources to support collaborative professional learning; provide professional learning and ongoing support for principals and teacher leaders (coaches) on leading, facilitating, supporting, and monitoring collaborative professional learning teams; develop and support teacher leaders (coaches) to facilitate learning teams; coordinate ongoing cross-school collaboration to share successes and address challenges.	Allocate resources to support collaborative professional learning; provide professional learning and ongoing support for principals and teacher leaders (coaches) on leading, facilitating, supporting, and monitoring collaborative professional learning teams; develop and support teacher leaders (coaches) to facilitate learning teams.	Provide professional learning and ongoing support for principals and teacher leaders (coaches) on leading, facilitating, supporting, and monitoring collaborative professional learning teams, and develop and support teacher leaders (coaches) to facilitate learning teams.	Endorse collaborative professional learning without providing specific support to schools.

TOOL INDEX

TOOL	TITLE	USE
14.1	8 smooth steps	Tool 14.1 provides a comprehensive overview of a process for evaluating professional learning.
14.2	Team meetings	Tool 14.2 is a brief survey for team members about the effectiveness of their team meetings.
14.3	Rate yourself as a team player	Tool 14.3 is a survey about team members' roles.
14.4	Protocol for discussing survey results about team effectiveness and/or team meetings	Tool 14.4 is a protocol for discussing data collected on one of the surveys included in this chapter's tools.
14.5	Learning School Innovation Configuration Map	Tool 14.5 is a tool for self-assessment and planning to implement NSDC's definition of professional learning.
14.6	Logic model template	Tool 14.6 is a template for creating a team's or school's own logic model for collaborative professional learning.
14.7	Learning team survey	Tool 14.7 is a survey for assessing a learning team.
14.8	Summative reflection protocol	Tool 14.8 is a protocol to guide team discussion about the team's summative evaluation.
14.9	Professional learning communities: Getting started	Tool 14.9 is a brief survey on the early implementation of a collaborative professional learning team.
14.10	Professional learning communities II: A focus on common assessments	Tool 14.10 is a survey on the more sophisticated implementation of collaborative professional learning teams.
14.11	Individual contribution protocol	Tool 14.11 is a protocol for more advanced learning teams to use about individual members' contributions.

PART 4

Engaging community

Chapter 15

COMMUNICATING
progress

WHERE ARE WE NOW?

The school leadership team engages facilitators and members of collaborative professional learning teams in discussing the teams' professional learning and its impact on student achievement.

STRONGLY AGREE   AGREE   NO OPINION   DISAGREE   STRONGLY DISAGREE

Each staff member takes responsibility to be an advocate of collaborative professional learning.

STRONGLY AGREE   AGREE   NO OPINION   DISAGREE   STRONGLY DISAGREE

We invite parents to participate in collaborative professional learning teams as appropriate.

STRONGLY AGREE   AGREE   NO OPINION   DISAGREE   STRONGLY DISAGREE

We share our successes and challenges with district staff.

STRONGLY AGREE   AGREE   NO OPINION   DISAGREE   STRONGLY DISAGREE

We regularly engage parents and the community in conversations about collaborative professional learning occurring in teams within the school and its impact on student learning.

STRONGLY AGREE   AGREE   NO OPINION   DISAGREE   STRONGLY DISAGREE

The elementary school posted a clear message on its marquee: "No school today. Teachers are learning."

The assumption that students have to be sent home to allow for teacher learning has existed in the design of school schedules for many years. For years, state and local policy makers have grappled with the number of days to include in a school calendar or to set as a minimum or maximum for professional development. These periodic inservice or professional development days scattered throughout the calendar send the message to parents — and even to teachers themselves — that adult learning does not occur on any other day of the school year.

Changing that message is essential to bringing about a more successful form of learning. How districts and schools communicate about collaborative professional learning matters immensely. "Schools where teachers focus on student work, interact with colleagues to plan how to improve their teaching, and continuously bring new skills and knowledge to bear on their practice are also schools that produce the best results for children. To make this level of achievement a reality in every school, the public first must be convinced that schools should be places where teachers as well as children learn" (NEA Foundation, 2000).

WHAT IS COMMUNICATED

Teachers first must get on board with a clear understanding of the benefits of collaborative professional learning. How educators understand the role of professional learning in improving student learning and communicate that to parents and the school community matters in how the public views professional learning.

"Survey after survey confirms that parents' No. 1 source of information on schools is teachers. Teachers must hold this trust in high regard," says Stephanie Hirsh, NSDC's executive director. "As a result, teachers are the most reliable source of information for parents about why collaborative learning is essential and how it benefits all students as well as the entire teaching staff. When talking to parents about professional learning, teachers should explain that, even though they have college degrees, they still have much to learn so that students achieve success. Professional development is the only means teachers have to improve their practices so that all students achieve their full potential" (personal communication, May 10, 2009).

A study of schools that won the U.S. Department of Education's National Award for Model Professional Development found that teachers failed to identify their extensive informal learning (Killion, 1999). Opportunities such as a having a writer in residence, meeting with colleagues to plan instruction, or working to solve problems related to student learning were not described as professional learning. Workshops both in and out of the school, summer courses, conferences, and university courses were recognized as professional learning. This finding has two interpretations. First, informal learning occurs naturally within schools, continuously contributing to refined practice. However, if teachers fail to acknowledge that they are learning and the learning has little impact on their practice or student learning, it contributes little value and the public has no reason to support further professional learning of the same kind.

Educators should develop well-constructed rationale with sound explanation about what they are learning and how it connects to student achievement. Linda Freeman, in an article in *Education Week*, suggests, "Considering the messages parents are hearing and the perceptions about education they are forming, educators who want to try to do things in a different way must be able to articulate why any changes are necessary, describe how the new strategies will work, and address the particular things about which parents are concerned. We must make the language of education clear and free of jargon. We must constantly remind ourselves that parents have different perceptions about education. The word 'reform' may mean something different in a different context to each parent. Everyone can agree that education needs to be improved; it is crucially important to involve everyone in an informed debate about how that is to be done."

Freeman offers these tips for speaking to the community about any school reform effort:

- Acknowledge that community members are bringing their own thoughts, feelings, and experiences about education to the reform process. Look for ways to make their backgrounds contribute positively to their understanding, just as teachers do with students.

- Clearly understand the goals of the reform effort. Educators are much less likely to become defensive if the goals they are describing are clearly defensible.

- Use interactions with other professionals as learning experiences — both good and bad. Pay attention to the words, tone, and body language those in the legal, medical, financial, and other professions use in their communications and gauge people's reactions.

- Be approachable and accessible. The "just enough — just in time" guideline works as effectively in talking with community members as it does with talking to students (Freeman, 1996).

> Educators should develop well-constructed rationale with sound explanation about what they are learning and how it connects to student achievement.

HOW THE MESSAGE IS COMMUNICATED

How the communication is structured also matters. In its report on engaging the public, the National Education Association Foundation included guidelines for school communications. "If communications are treated as a one-way transmission of information from the school to the public, then other interactions between the schools and the public are likely to remain one-way, as well. Effective communications rely on a model of continuous feedback, wherein audiences are encouraged to react to information they receive, and the author (e.g. the school or district) visibly incorporates that response into the next communication or ac-

TIPS FOR GAINING SUPPORT

Teachers, principals, central office staff, superintendents, and school board members have a role in advocating for and supporting professional learning. To achieve support:

1. Meet with education reporters to discuss the role of professional learning in its improvement plan and in helping the district achieve its goals.

2. Ask teachers to write a regular column or editorial for the local newspaper about their professional learning or to use Web 2.0 tools such as discussion groups, blogs, or Twitter to share their experiences.

3. Invite parents to participate in collaborative learning teams as appropriate so they can understand more deeply how the time is used and how it contributes to student learning.

4. Create learning communities for parents and community members on issues related to family involvement in student academic success.

5. Meet with community groups such as Rotary, Lions Club, Chamber of Commerce, Business Roundtable, etc., to discuss the role of continuous improvement in educators' development.

6. Draw parallels between training and development expectations from business and industry, such as those embedded in the Baldrige Award or International Organization for Standardization — certification to help community members and parents understand the value of ongoing educator development.

7. Work with community agencies to provide cocurricular programs for students so instructional time is not reduced during teachers' collaborative time.

8. Give parents information about the work of individual teams and their findings.

9. Develop laser talks for educators to use in talking about their own professional development, its benefits, and their role in making decisions about their professional learning.

10. Encourage educators to speak positively, yet honestly, with parents and community members about their professional learning.

tion," the report states. **Table 15.1** describes these differences.

WHERE AND TO WHOM TO COMMUNICATE

To keep communication flowing between and among those engaged in collaborative professional learning and those who have an interest in it, all stakeholders should make an effort to communicate frequently. Sometimes that communication is one-way, such as when a principal writes about teams' work in the parent newsletter. More often communication is two-way, such as when the principal meets with team facilitators to learn about each team's progress and to share data from new district benchmark assessments. At other times, communication involves multiple groups, such as when the school leadership team hosts a meeting for parents, community members, and district office staff to meet with team leaders, the coach, and team members to learn more about the changed school schedule that allows time for collaboration within the workday.

School leadership teams, particularly principals

Table 15.1 TYPES OF COMMUNICATION

	Monologue	**Dialogue**	**Engagement**
Process	One-way talking or "informing," with no suggested action on the part of the audience.	Two-way communication, inviting initial participation by the audience.	Two-way communication, incorporating results from previous interactions and suggesting a new course of action.
Message	"Our teachers need more professional development."	"Join us for a meeting to discuss how teacher learning affects student learning, and explore options for our teachers to update their skills and knowledge."	"Please come to a follow-up forum to examine the draft plan for district professional development for next year and talk about strategies for the upcoming referendum on changing the elementary school calendar."

Source: NEA Foundation, 2000, www.neafoundation.org/publications/engaging.htm#tipsback

who communicate often with teams, focus on collaborative professional learning goals and the benefits to students. **Table 15.2** is a list of some of the various communication exchanges that support collaborative professional learning.

SHAPING THE IMAGE

Each educator shares responsibility for shaping the school community's image about professional learning. Language used to talk about professional learning makes a difference. An exasperated parent in one district, faced with a "professional development day" for which she needed to find child care, asked, "Why do teachers need special days called workdays? Don't they work every day? Is a workday supposed to be more work than a regular day of work?"

Parents who work in the business arena can't comprehend shutting down the office for a day to provide staff training. In most businesses, employees take part in ongoing training and development without any disruption of business. Even dentists and physicians who leave their office to participate in ongoing professional

REFLECTIONS

1. What are our typical communications like — monologue, dialogue, or engagement? What underlying beliefs and assumptions lead us to our preferred method of communicating?

2. What are our fundamental beliefs about the role of professional learning in student achievement?

3. How do we communicate the relationship between professional learning and student learning to parents and the school community?

4. How can we eliminate the perception that for teachers to learn, students must stop learning?

5. What improvements can we make in our communication to parents about professional development?

learning have staff or support to ensure that patient care is not interrupted. For educators, team meetings should be part of the natural workday.

Shaping that perception is educators' job. Parents pay close attention to what educators say and want to support their schools' teachers. How schools communicate about their continuous improvement work is as important a matter as establishing the structures and systems for collaboration.

REFERENCES

Freeman, L. (1996, November 6). Talking to parents about school reform. *Education Week.* Available at www.edweek.org/ew/articles/1996/11/06/10freem.h16.html?tkn=YPRF92zCxrFXiLnuObl2Vw72rECgeh4KmsLR&print=1.

Killion, J. (1999). *Islands of hope in a sea of dreams: A research report on the eight schools that received the National Award for Model Professional Development.* San Francisco: WestEd.

NEA Foundation. (2000). *Engaging public support for teachers' professional development overview.* Available at www.neafoundation.org/publications/engaging.htm#tipsback.

Table 15.2 TYPES OF COMMUNICATION EXCHANGES

Who communicates	To whom	About	When
Principals	Faculty	• Expectation for participation • Purpose of collaborative professional learning • School goals • Student data • Progress toward goals • Team strategies and successes	Weekly at first; several times per school year after established
	School leadership team	• Expectations for participation • Student achievement data • Team goals for professional learning and student achievement • Vision for school success • Resources allocated to collaborative professional learning • Challenges to overcome	Monthly
	Team facilitators	• Team goals for professional learning and student achievement • Student achievement data • Strategies for improving team learning, processes, and results • Learning from other teams	Monthly
	Coaches	• Plan to support teams • Strategies used to support teams and individual teachers • Type of support provided to teams and individual teachers • Plan for additional professional learning	Weekly
	Parents and community members	• School goals • Team goals • Progress toward goals • Benefits of collaboration • Results from collaborative professional learning • Parent concerns about schedule	Monthly
School leadership team, principal, teacher leaders, and maybe representatives from district office and community	Faculty	• Purpose of collaboration	When beginning collaborative professional learning
	Teams	• Their goals	Several times per school year
	Team facilitators	• Progress of the team's work • School goals and strategies for accomplishing them • Team goals and strategies for accomplishing them	Several times per school year
	Coaches	• School goals and strategies for accomplishing them • Team goals and strategies for accomplishing them • Support coaches provide • Progress toward school goals • Additional strategies for team learning or work	Monthly

Table 15.2 TYPES OF COMMUNICATION EXCHANGES, continued

Who communicates	To whom	About	When
School leadership team, principal, teacher leaders, and maybe representatives from district office and community	District staff	• Schoolwide goals • Team goals • Data about student performance • Strategies for developing faculty capacity to engage in collaborative professional learning	Several times per year
	Parents and community members	• Value of collaborative professional learning • Benefits for students • Work of the teams • Progress toward the school's goals	Frequently when initiating collaborative professional learning and at least twice a year each year of implementation
Coaches	Team facilitators	• Agenda for team meetings • Strategies and resources for accomplishing team goals • Refinements to team processes	Weekly or more often
	Individual teachers	• Support for and feedback on implementing learning and interventions in the classroom • Adaptations to meet specific student learning needs • Resources to support implementation • Additional professional learning • Student progress toward benchmarks	Weekly
Team facilitators	Team members	• Changes in team structure, agenda, or processes • Requests for engagement • Opportunities for extended learning • Feedback on team meetings	Once a month or more frequently
	District staff members	• Requests for resources or support • Requests for additional learning on curriculum • Assessment, instruction, working with students with special learning needs	As needed
Individual teachers	Team facilitator	• Challenges associated with the team meeting • Requests for support from the team • Opportunities for extended professional learning	As needed
	Coach	• Requests for classroom support • Requests for resources • Assistance with planning and teaching	As needed

TOOL INDEX

TOOL	TITLE	USE
15.1	Delivering a laser talk	Tool 15.1 offers a framework for advocating for effective professional learning, with an example of how to advocate for NSDC's definition of professional development.
15.2	Engaging public support for teachers' professional development overview	Tool 15.2 provides guidelines for engaging parents and the public in supporting teacher professional learning and can be downloaded, read, and discussed. Available at www.neafoundation.org/publications/engaging.htm#tipsback.
15.3	*JSD* Forum: Parents and teachers need to know	Tool 15.3 summarizes parents' and teachers' needs related to professional development.

JOELLEN KILLION

Joellen Killion is deputy executive director of the National Staff Development Council, where she focuses on improving teaching quality and student learning. She has been director of NSDC's highly acclaimed NSDC Academy and its Coaches Academy for school-based staff developers. She also has managed numerous projects, including NSDC's initiatives in results-based

staff development, evaluating staff development, and Results Skills for School Leaders project.

Killion is the author of *Assessing Impact: Evaluating Staff Development,* 2nd ed. (Corwin Press & NSDC, 2008), co-author with Stephanie Hirsh of *The Learning Educator: A New Era for Professional Learning* (NSDC, 2007) and with Cindy Harrison of *Taking the Lead: New Roles for Teachers and School-Based Coaches* (NSDC, 2006). She authored NSDC's *What Works* series (2001), which summarizes studies of content-specific staff development for various grade levels. She was featured in the School Improvement Network/VideoJournal programs *Instructional Coaching* and *Designing and Evaluating Professional Development.*

Her examination of schools that received the U.S. Department of Education's National Award for Model Professional Development resulted in the publication of *Teachers Who Learn, Kids Who Achieve: A Look at Model Professional Development* (WestEd, 2000). She is also the author of *E-Learning for Educators: Implementing the Standards* (NSDC & NICI, 2000).

Killion is a former school district staff developer, curriculum coordinator, and teacher in the Adams 12 Five Star School District in suburban Denver. She was a member of NSDC's Board of Trustees and served a term as president. She lives in suburban Denver.

PATRICIA ROY

Patricia Roy is a national education consultant living in Arizona. She is the author of many articles and chapters on cooperative learning, effective professional development, and school improvement. She served on both committees to develop and revise NSDC's Standards for Staff Development and co-authored with Shirley Hord *Moving NSDC's Staff Development Standards Into Practice: Innovation Configurations, Vol. I & II* (2003 & 2005). She also is the author of *User's Guide: Innovation Configurations for NSDC's Standards for Staff Development* (NSDC, 2007) and *Training Manual: NSDC's Standards for Staff Development* (NSDC, 2006). For sev-

eral years, she has written monthly columns on standards for two NSDC newsletters, *The Learning Principal* and *The Learning System.*

She was the founding director of the Delaware Professional Development Center, which focused on school improvement for student achievement. She served as director of the Center for School Change at Delaware State University through an SSI grant from the National Science Foundation. She has been a teacher, cooperative learning consultant, a district staff development coordinator in Arizona, and an administrator in a Minnesota regional educational agency. Roy served on NSDC's Board of Trustees and was president in 1992. She received NSDC's Best Dissertation award for her work focusing on an evaluation of a district professional development program.